THE SUNDAY TIMES
Shopping Online

THE SUNDAY TIMES
Shopping Online

Matthew Wall

HarperCollins*Publishers*

Matthew Wall is a freelance journalist and TV research/producer best-known for his weekly *Web Wise* internet column in *The Sunday Times*. He also writes internet features for the paper's Culture section and has written several internet reports for business. He also advises companies on web design and strategy.

HarperCollins Publishers
77-85 Fulham Palace Road
Hammersmith
London W6 8JB

fireand**water**.com
Visit the book lover's website

First published 2000

Reprint 10 9 8 7 6 5 4 3 2 1 0

© Times Newspapers Ltd 2000

ISBN   0 7230 1074 9

Designer: Sylvie Rabbe
Layout: Beatrice Waller
Editor: Sarah Barlow

Designed, edited and typeset by Book Creation Services Ltd.

Printed in Great Britain by Omnia Books Ltd, Glasgow G64

Contents

Acknowledgments

I would like to thank all those who helped me in the preparation of this guide, not least the hundreds of *Sunday Times* readers who have shared their online shopping experiences with me; my wife, Wendy, for her patience; and Christopher Riches at HarperCollins for his refreshingly subtle editorial touch.

Matthew Wall

May 2000

Acknowledgements

Getting Started

Introduction

Welcome to *The Sunday Times Shopping Online*. We tell you everything you need to know to help you find those online bargains, and give you plenty of advice on how to shop safely and securely.

This guide assumes that you are already pretty familiar with internet basics. If you're not, try *The Sunday Times Guide to the Internet* for starters. It will give you a good grounding in how the web works so that you can make the most of what's on offer.

We'll take you through the pros and cons of shopping online, telling you how to do it, pointing out the potential pitfalls as well as the advantages. We recommend good sites to shop at and offer tips on how to protect yourself online. Above all, we give you practical advice, not theoretical blurb. We've tested out lots of online retailers at home and abroad and we've received e-mails from hundreds of people who've done likewise.

This isn't just a guide full of web addresses that could go out of date very quickly. It has been designed to give you the necessary tools so that you can adapt to the net's rapidly

1

changing environment with confidence. The net is just a tool – a telephone with big pretensions. There's no need to be intimidated by it. So let's cut a swathe through all that net-nerd jargon and the marketing hype and make the net work for you, saving you time and money.

Shopping online: just the beginning ...

These days it seems you can buy anything online, from novelty soap to luxury cars. Most things that you can buy in the shops you can also buy on the net. It's only just taking off, and yet it's already massive. In the US, where online shopping is well established, over 28 million households will shop online in 2000, and 11 million of these will do it for the first time, according to Forrester Research, a US research consultancy. Not a week goes by without some research company coming out with another astronomical forecast for the amount we're going to spend online over the next few years.

Although the US may be ahead of the game for the time being, we Europeans are beginning to catch up after a slow start. Experts believe our online spending will increase thirteen-fold to around £28 billion by 2002. And it's the UK that's leading the European pack. Pollster NOP estimates that we will spend more than £10 billion online in the year 2000. That's an absolutely massive amount considering that we only spent around £3.2 billion the year before, and less than £500 million the year before that. No wonder there are so many net-related adverts on TV these days. Around four million of the UK's 13 million net users have shopped online so far, but the number is rising fast. The lure of the web is proving irresistible.

But before we get carried away, maybe we should put all this into context. Online shopping isn't about to turn our city centres into ghost towns. At least, not yet. In the UK online consumer spending is still less than 5% of the amount we spend in the high street. In Europe as a whole the figure is less than 1%. But what is remarkable is the speed with which these figures are rising.

What are we buying?

In these early days of shopping online we're understandably a little nervous about spending too much. The main – almost completely unfounded – fear holding people back is that their credit card details will be stolen and misused. So it comes as no surprise that the most popular items being bought are books, CDs, videos, and computer software – relatively low-value goods that you don't have to try out before you buy. And if it all goes horribly wrong, you haven't lost much.

> **FACT**
>
> *In the UK online consumer spending is still less than 5% of the amount we spend in the high street.*

What tends to happen is that online shoppers start off with small purchases, to test the system, then if all goes well, they spend a little more and a little more often. It's all about building confidence. Once shoppers feel safe, and they realise their credit card bills aren't full of fraudulent transactions, their online shopping activity accelerates as they take advantage of all the net can offer.

These days people are being a lot more adventurous – buying holidays, cinema tickets, cars, groceries, wine, clothes. You name it, people are buying it online. And as web retailers improve their sites and level of customer service, confidence is growing and the opportunities for online commerce are expanding daily.

Is it all good news?

One of the reasons online shopping has had a slow start relative to other net activities such as e-mail is that web retailers have struggled to get to grips with the new electronic medium. When you sell online your website is your shop front. It's your main link to your customers. Yet many retailers still put up sites that are difficult to use, have miniscule photographs, and do more to put people off than to attract their custom.

One thing online shoppers need far more than their 'bricks-and-mortar' counterparts is reassurance. Shopping online is a strange and forbidding experience for many. They want to know exactly who it is they're dealing with and how they can contact them if they need help. Again, many retailers provide almost no contact details or even fail to tell online customers who they are. This hardly inspires confidence. Even when they do supply contact details, many retailers completely underestimate the net's power to attract business. They don't staff their online operations sufficiently, leading to poor customer service. Unacknowledged e-mail is one of the most common complaints from online shoppers and net users in general.

Finally, once you've got past the technology bit, there's still the age-old problem of delivering the right goods to the right property, intact and on time. Stories abound of Christmas presents being delivered late or not at all, of inaccurate grocery orders including foods that weren't ordered. This isn't specifically a net problem: it has bedevilled all mail-order retailers for years. Many new online retailers have simply been swamped by demand and have failed to sort out the logistics of the business before launching their websites.

Even in the US, where online shopping is most advanced, services are far from flawless. According to the Boston Consulting Group, a US research company, at least four out of five online shoppers have experienced one failed purchase and 28% of all online purchases fail. The most common problems are websites that take too long to load, sites that are so badly designed that products can't be found, and delivery delays.

The main concern for retailers is that the net has heightened customer expectations considerably. We expect digital information to be delivered online at the speed of light, and have come to expect real-world goods to be delivered almost as quickly. Online shoppers are a pretty intolerant bunch. One unhappy experience can put people off shopping online for good and, at the least, stop them coming back to a particular retailer.

One reason why online shopping has been slower to take off in Europe compared to the US is internet access costs. Although most internet service providers have now stopped charging monthly membership fees, surveys show that online shopping would grow much faster if net users weren't continually worrying about high telephone charges. According to Durlacher Research, a UK company, home net users would increase the number of times they go online by 46% if they weren't charged by the minute but had unmetered access for a fixed fee instead. Luckily this is beginning to happen.

Another problem that frustrates people and restricts the online shopping experience is slow internet connections. For most of us, the fastest we can download data, images and sound is 56 kilobits per second – the speed of the fastest modem. This means that downloading video snippets and music samples longer than a few seconds takes ages. Many shoppers just give up in frustration.

Clearly, if you want to buy clothes online, anything that gives you a more complete picture of how the clothes look and move is going to be welcome. Short videos will help retailers enormously. But until we get high-speed connections, whether through cable modems or through new technologies such as ADSL (Asynchronous Digital Subscriber Line), we'll just have to make do. Such high-speed alternatives are coming soon, but they're unlikely to be cheap.

So why bother shopping online?

After reading the above you may wonder whether shopping online is worth it! But this guide cuts through the hype and tells you what life on the net is really like. It's not perfect by any means, but it is getting better, and the pros outweigh the cons. So what are the pros?

FACT

According to Durlacher Research, a UK company, home net users would increase the number of times they go online by 46% if they weren't charged by the minute but had unmetered access for a fixed fee instead. Luckily this is beginning to happen.

Convenience

At this stage, convenience is the main advantage of shopping online. The net never shuts, so you can shop online at 3am if you like. You don't have to worry about rushing out in your lunch hour and trying to buy everything you need before dashing back to work. No more struggling through traffic, arguing with traffic wardens or standing in bus queues in the rain. And what about that infuriating experience of battling through the Saturday crowds only to discover from some surly shop assistant that the very thing you want is out of stock? All that stress disappears.

You can do everything from the comfort of your own home at a time and a speed that suits you. There's a lot less pressure, apart from the niggling worry that you're running up a large phone bill as you peruse online shopping malls. But even this concern is fading as fixed-fee unlimited net access becomes the norm.

The net is especially convenient for those items that you have to buy rather than want to buy. Groceries fall into this category. Increasing numbers of people are happy to pay a premium for the added convenience of doing their food shopping online. Any parent who's dragged complaining kids round a superstore whilst being barged into by grumpy trolley-wielding grannies will fully appreciate the benefits the net can offer.

Cost

Although it's a mistake to assume that everything is cheaper on the net, many retailers are finding that they can undercut their competitors by offering goods online. After all, you don't need shops in high streets any more to reach a national audience. All you need is a website, a warehouse and an efficient delivery system. That cuts out a lot of the costs associated with running a traditional business. And this enables online retailers to offer lower prices to customers.

Much has been made of 'rip-off Britain' and the high prices we've been forced to pay for goods compared to our European or US

FACT

Many retailers are finding that they can undercut their competitors by offering goods online.

7

neighbours. The net is helping to introduce a welcome blast of competition into the high street and wake traditional retailers from their lethargy. Books, for example, have dropped remarkably in price since online retailers Amazon and BOL entered the market offering discounts of up to 50% on bestsellers. High street bookshops, like W H Smith and Waterstone's, have been forced to drop prices in response. Such competition has also accelerated their moves into online retailing.

Choice

The wonderful thing about the net's disregard for geographical boundaries is that a whole new world of choice opens up to the online shopper. Goods and services which might have been hard to come by in your local town are now just a click away. And we're not just talking about the UK. You can shop globally these days, buying from merchants in Singapore or Sydney, Manchester or Minneapolis. The net is opening up a truly global marketplace and there are lots of bargains to be found shopping abroad (*see* **Shopping Abroad**, *page 83*), even after taking VAT and import duties into account.

FACT

Goods and services which might have been hard to come by in your local town are now just a click away.

But I keep hearing that shopping online is risky. Is it?

No it isn't, not if you're careful. Shopping online using your credit card is a lot safer than buying things over the phone and certainly no riskier than handing your credit card over in a restaurant, say. The main fear – that your credit card details may be stolen and you could lose a lot of money – is unfounded. The misconception arises partly from a lack of understanding about encryption – the process of scrambling your card details according to a complex mathematical formula before they are sent across the network. This means that any hacker who was lucky enough to intercept your details in transit would be extremely hard-pressed to decipher the code.

Even then your liability for so-called 'card-not-present' fraud is restricted to £50 in most cases, provided you haven't been negligent. And in fact, as long as you report any suspicious transactions as soon as you notice them, most card providers won't hold you liable at all. More and more credit card companies are now promising automatic refunds if customers are defrauded whilst using their credit cards online.

There are more legitimate concerns about retailers' own security arrangements and how they handle your personal data. But for more on this and how to shop safely and securely online, *see* **Safe Shopping**, *page 21.*

TIP

Shopping online using your credit card is a lot safer than buying things over the phone and certainly no riskier than handing your credit card over in a restaurant.

TIP

Liability for so-called 'card-not-present' fraud is restricted to £50 in most cases, provided you haven't been negligent.

Chapter 2

How do I do It?

The essential tools

As we said in the introduction, this guide assumes you have some basic knowledge about the net and how it works, so we don't need to go into too much detail here. But obviously you need:

1. a computer (the faster the better)

2. a modem (the faster the better)

3. an internet service provider (preferably one that offers unlimited access for a fixed annual or monthly fee)

4. the latest version web browser

It is quite important to get an up-to-date version of a web browser, because they have the very latest security features incorporated. These include the ability to handle various forms of encryption, so that you can send your credit card details across the net safely, and sophisticated filtering tools to help screen out websites that may not be safe or trustworthy. You can also set your browser security settings to accept or reject cookies – small text files retailers and other

11

service providers sometimes download on to your hard drive to help them identify you and your surfing habits. For more on this, *see* **Safe Shopping**, *page 21.*

Equip yourself with some useful programs

Web retailers are improving the quality of their sites all the time. Surfing can now be a rich multimedia experience incorporating sound, images, video and animation. But to make the most of all of this you need the right software. These programs are called plug-ins, despite the fact that they don't actually plug in.

The latest versions of web browsers have several useful plug-ins already incorporated, but you don't have to stick with these. A popular program for music and video, and the one that seems to be dominating the market, is **RealPlayer** (**www.real.com**), which includes RealAudio and RealVideo. Microsoft has its own version called Windows Media Player incorporated into Internet Explorer. Apple's version is called **QuickTime** (**www.apple.com/quicktime**).

Other important programs are **Shockwave** and **Flash** (**www.shockwave.com**) from Macromedia, which enable your browser to handle animated graphics and other advanced website design features. A lot of websites are using this program these days, so if you don't have it, your browser won't be able to load the page properly. Usually, if this happens, the website provides a link to the software company so that you can download the required software there and then.

The only snag is that some of these programs can be several Megabytes in size and take a long time to download, especially with a slow modem (28.8kbps) and at a busy time of the day. Instead, download software

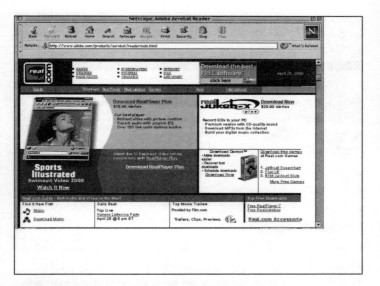

RealPlayer (www.real.com) is the leading plug-in for music and video.

early in the morning (when most Americans are still in bed), or look out for free CD-ROMS accompanying net and PC magazines. These often have useful plug-ins on them and it takes a fraction of the time loading them on to your hard drive.

Another useful program is **Adobe Acrobat Reader** (**www.adobe.com**). A lot of documents on the web are now designed using Adobe Acrobat, which helps make pages look exactly as they would in a conventional book or magazine. But you need the Acrobat Reader plug-in to read these files

TIP

Keep your browser up-to-date so it can handle the latest website design features.

(called PDF files). It is well worth getting, especially if you plan to print off documents – the quality is excellent. Also,

13

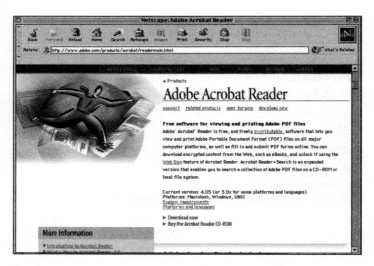

Many pages on the web are created as PDF files, which allows them to keep their original design and fonts. But you need the Acrobat Reader plug-in to view and print them.

websites often have forms that you need to fill in. Rather than completing them online, you can print them off before posting.

Some websites may also use mini-programs called ActiveX controls and Java Applets. Active X controls are stored on your computer, Java Applets aren't. They may also use advanced programming languages, such as JavaScript. The main problem is that these latest website design features can only be handled by the latest web browsers. Earlier browser versions sometimes cannot load pages designed using these programs and languages. This is another reason why you have to keep your browser up-to-date (but be aware that a very new browser often has security holes). You may also need to tweak your browser security settings to allow such advanced features to be downloaded.

The online shopping process

First, find an online retailer . . . There's tons of information on good places to start and excellent sites to visit in Chapters 4, 5 and 8. Where you start largely depends on whether you know what you're looking for. It's quite usual to have to register on the website first. This usually involves giving your name, e-mail address and other contact details. So long as this isn't too onerous or intrusive, registration can be useful. It helps the website to recognize you when you return, and also to send you e-mails targeted at your particular interests.

You don't have to be online while filling in the form. Just log off until you've completed it. When you press the 'Submit' or similar button your browser should automatically reconnect you. If you still pay per-minute net call charges, this is a useful way of saving money on your phone bill.

Have a look at what's on offer . . . Retailers organize their products in a whole host of ways, some more logical than others. But basically you browse through an online equivalent of a mail-order catalogue. There are usually photographs accompanying product descriptions, although these can sometimes be very small. This is especially unhelpful on clothes sites, where you really want to get a close look at the materials.

One major advantage of the net over traditional forms of retailing is the amount of information you can supply with the products. For example, book sites often include reviews from people who've read the book you're interested in, or forums to discuss views on books with other readers. CD retailers will often supply snippets of music to help you decide whether you want to buy a particular album.

It's also very easy to search for what you want on the website. Most sites include a search engine so that you can just type in what you're looking for and it will take you straight there. This can save a lot of time browsing.

Select something to buy . . . If you find something you want to buy, you click on an icon that says 'Add to basket' or 'Add to trolley', using a supermarket analogy. You can usually enter the number of items you want in a box headed 'Quantity'. You can add as many separate items to your basket as you like while you're browsing. And if you change your mind, it's very easy to delete an item you don't want. At this stage you haven't committed yourself to anything.

Flash the plastic . . . Once you've finished browsing and you want to go ahead and buy, you proceed to what most websites call the 'Checkout' or something similar connected to the 'real' world. This is where you check that your order is accurate and that you've specified the right quantities. The site will usually work out the total cost for you, including delivery.

> **TIP**
>
> *You can normally tell when you're in secure mode when you see the web address at the top of your browser window change to begin https://. At the bottom of your browser window you should also see a locked padlock symbol, an unbroken key, or some other icon, depending on the type of browser you have.*

If you're happy to proceed, it's time to wield the plastic and enter your credit card details. Some sites will also accept debit cards. At this stage a website will often give you the option to go to 'secure mode', if you haven't been directed there automatically. Once you're in this mode, any data going to and from your computer to the retailer's computers is encrypted. Your transaction is safe from prying eyes.

You can normally tell when you're in secure mode when you see the web address at the top of your browser window change to begin **https://**. At the bottom of your browser window you should also see a locked padlock symbol or some other icon, depending on the type of browser you have. If you're scrupulous about security, you should never send your credit card details to a computer server that doesn't have an encrypted connection. I must confess that I have without suffering any ill effects, but I try not to make a habit of it.

Even at this very late stage you haven't bought anything until you click on the button saying 'Submit', 'Place order' or something similar. There's still time to change your mind if you get cold feet. But once you've clicked on that button there's no going back...

Order confirmation . . . Good retail websites will send you an instant e-mail detailing the order, as well as confirming it on the website itself. Make sure you keep this e-mail as proof that you made the purchase, and print off the website confirmation page as well just to be on the safe side. Computers do crash from time to time and e-mails can get wiped, so old-fashioned paper-based back-up is a good idea.

Order tracking . . . Some websites will also let you track the progress of your order if you log on to the website. The correct web page address is often included in the e-mail. Again, it is good practice for the web retailer to e-mail you when the product is actually despatched, keeping you up-to-date with developments. Obviously, not all websites live up to these high standards of customer service and you should try to find out as much as possible about the company's policies regarding post-sales care before you buy.

Await delivery . . . After this relatively simple process, you
then wait for your goods to arrive – hopefully accurately
processed and on time. If you're buying from abroad, this can
take several weeks. Domestic deliveries can take just a few
days. The whole online shopping process can be extremely
quick. I once researched and bought a new washing machine
online in 15 minutes flat, saving £100 on high-street prices
into the bargain. Of course, making a process easy can be a
mixed blessing, especially if you're a shopaholic with a
tendency to be profligate with your plastic!

A word about delivery charges

Some web retailers can be a little parsimonious when it
comes to information on delivery charges. But it is very
important. Any difference between online and high-street
prices can be wiped out by the added cost of delivery. So
make sure you find out exactly what the costs are before
committing yourself.

Obviously the total
delivery charge will vary
according to the quantity
and type of goods you
buy. It is often calculated
only at the very end of the
process, once you've entered your card details. But as
mentioned above, you can still go this far without committing
yourself to anything. It's only when you click on the 'Place
order' button that you actually make the purchase.

So if you think the delivery costs are too high, cancel the
operation. One of the main advantages of the net is that
there's no pressure selling. You're in control all the time and
there's no queue of shoppers tutting impatiently behind you.

> **TIP**
>
> *It's only when you click on the 'Place
> order' button that you actually make the
> purchase.*

Web retailers have cottoned on to the fact that shoppers are concerned not only about product prices but also about delivery costs. Clarifying, or even removing, delivery costs certainly makes the whole process more straightforward. CD retailers in particular have felt compelled to consider this as they were facing intense competition from US retailers. You could buy CDs from the US more cheaply than in the UK, even after taking delivery charges into account.

Removing delivery costs in the UK helps to restore a level playing field. Music lovers may be tempted to spend a little more at a UK site if they know they're likely to get their CDs earlier than if they buy from abroad. When you make a purchase from a foreign website, true price comparisons are made more difficult if you have to include VAT and import duty in the equation. You don't always have to, but *see* **Shopping Abroad**, *page 83* for more information.

Chapter 3

Safe Shopping

Exploding the myths

Survey after survey finds that security is the still the biggest issue preventing more people from shopping online. But it's a Catch-22 situation. Those who've never shopped online won't because they're worried that if they give out their credit card details calamitous things will happen. But they won't know that this is most unlikely until they start shopping online. The key is to give people the confidence to make that first purchase. Once the ice has been broken there's usually no stopping them.

The situation is not helped by a media more interested in whipping up a good net scare story than reporting the mundane truth. Shopping online is as safe, if not safer, that other forms of shopping, particularly shopping by telephone. If you believed most of the stories around you would think the world was plagued by rampaging hackers and fraudsters, stealing your credit card details, breaking into your computers and causing general mayhem. This just isn't the case. There are very few cases of fraud involving stolen credit card details, especially when you consider that there are

Card issuers such as Egg (www.egg.com) offer fraud guarantees, promising to stand any loss the customer incurs through fraud on the web.

approaching 250 million people worldwide with net access nowadays.

Yes, there have been some alarming cases of retail websites being breached by hackers and credit card numbers being publicly posted on the web. But most of the time this kind of stunt is pulled by hackers wanting to show how clever they are and to point out security flaws in retailers' computer systems. In a way, benign hackers are doing us a favour if they force companies to improve the levels of protection they provide for our personal and confidential details.

And anyway, people also forget that the problem of net credit card fraud is not really our problem: it's the card issuers' problem. Nine times out of ten we won't be held liable if fraudulent purchases are made using our card details without our knowledge. So long as we haven't been negligent, our liability is restricted to £50. And in most cases, the card issuer accepts full liability anyway, even if you've shopped at foreign websites. The credit card market is very competitive at the moment. Card issuers don't want to risk losing customers by penalizing them for something that wasn't their fault.

Some card issuers, such as **Egg** (**www.egg.com**), **Marbles** (**www.getmarbles.com**) and **Barclaycard** (**www.barclaycard.co.uk**), offer fraud guarantees with their cards, promising to stand any loss the customer incurs through fraud on the web. This is a clever marketing gimmick, given the continuing level of concern about security. But there's no real need to get such a card just for this reason. Using a credit card online gives you *increased* protection, but more of that later.

> **TIP**
>
> *Shopping online is as safe, if not safer, that other forms of shopping, particularly shopping by telephone.*

How encryption works

Your credit card details are pretty safe when crossing an open network like the web because they are encrypted, providing you're connected to a computer capable of handling encryption, known as a secure server. Encryption is a way of scrambling information so that it can be transferred across an open network, such as the net, without anyone being able to understand what the message is. Only the intended recipient has the 'key' to unlock the code. The data is jumbled up according to a mathematical formula or algorithm and the way these rules are implemented depends on a what's called a 'cryptographic key', made up of a variable string of ones and noughts called bits.

The highest or strongest form of encryption available for web use has a 128-bit key. At the moment this is mainly restricted to financial websites, such as banks and stockbrokers. Shoppers generally have to make do with 40- or 56-bit encryption. These lower forms of encryption have been cracked by dedicated teams of people linking powerful computers together to crunch billions of numbers for hours and hours.

But don't let this worry you. The key to successful cryptography is not discovering a completely fool-proof code, but making it so difficult that it's not worth anyone's while to try to decode it. As long as the value of the prize is lower than the cost of winning it, encryption should deter criminals. A criminal who can easily get your credit card number from a carbon paper receipt in a shop or restaurant is hardly going to bother linking up 250 computers on the off-chance that he or she might intercept your number as it whizzes through cyberspace.

The most widespread forms of encryption rely on a system of unique digital keys for encoding and decoding the data or messages. One of the by-products of this is that it is also possible to use encryption as a way of verifying the identity of the sender, and that the message or data hasn't been tampered with in transit. This may involve loading digital certificates on to your computer that can then be used to encrypt messages going to those sites that own the certificates.

> **TIP**
>
> *Your credit card details are pretty safe when crossing an open network like the web because they are encrypted, providing you're connected to a computer capable of handling encryption, known as a secure server.*

But for day-to-day shopping on the net, a simple secure server that scrambles your card and personal details before transit is quite sufficient. Secure Sockets Layer (SSL) is the standard online payment security system developed by

Netscape for its Navigator web browser. Now it is the most widely used system and is supported by all the major browsers.

By and large you don't need to worry too much about the technical side of things. I know I don't. I've bought lots of things online and I've never been defrauded.

Understanding user names, passwords and cookies

When you register on a website – and you don't always have to – it involves choosing or being allocated a user name. It doesn't really matter what this is and it doesn't have to be your real name. If the website sends you e-mails, it will address you as your user name. If the website offers the opportunity to store personal information about you, it will also ask you to choose a password or a personal identification number that only you know. When you type in the password during the initial registration process it will only appear as a series of star symbols like this * * * * * *. As you won't know if you've typed it in correctly, most sites ask you to type it in again for confirmation.

Be careful when choosing your password, as some sites have different policies with regard to case-sensitivity. So if you have a lower-case password but accidentally press the 'Caps Lock' key on your keyboard before typing it in, it won't recognize you and you won't be able to access the site. It's quite common for sites to let you choose a reminder question in case you forget your password. It should go without saying that you shouldn't reveal your password to anybody or write it down in a publicly accessible place.

The main advantage of registering and divulging some personal information is that it helps the website tailor its service to your needs and let you know about special offers and promotions you might be interested in. Very often the retailer will place a small information file on your computer known as a **cookie**. This tells the retailer about you and records your movements around a website. The cookie can be updated each time you access the site, so that the retailer builds up a profile based on your tastes and behaviour. So if you often buy CDs in a particular style of music, the retailer can tell you about new releases in that same category, because it has a record of what you've bought.

Much has been made about the potential invasion of privacy from cookies. But they're generally harmless really. They're not active programs that could do nasty things to your hard drive and they can speed the whole logging on process by remembering who you are. You can also store your card and delivery address details so you don't need to type them in every time you want to make a purchase at your favourite website. This also saves a lot of time.

TIP

Be careful when choosing your password, as some sites have different policies with regard to case-sensitivity. So if you have a lower-case password but accidentally press the 'Caps Lock' key on your keyboard before typing it in, it won't recognise you and you won't be able to access the site.

If you still don't like the idea of cookies on your hard drive you can alter the security settings in your browser (providing you have the latest version – 4.x onwards for Netscape Navigator and Microsoft Internet Explorer). You're given the option to disable cookies completely or at least accept or reject them on an ad hoc basis. Bear in mind that some websites won't load properly or let you in at all without cookies being enabled. If you're surfing sites you don't know and don't necessarily trust yet, it can be a good idea to disable cookies in your security settings. If you trust the sites you're visiting, just enable them again.

The latest versions of operating systems also give you the option to save your password and user name so that when you want to access a site regularly, the security box pops up with the user name and password boxes already filled in. Of course, you shouldn't choose this option if other people have access to your computer. But it can save time.

How do I know if a website offers secure payments?

These days you're very unlikely to come across a retailer that doesn't offer secure trading. They realize that people just aren't going to buy from them unless they can convince customers that it is safe. So if they have any sense they'll advertise the safety aspects of their service very loudly. But you shouldn't take a website's word for it. Your web browser can tell you a great deal.

> **TIP**
>
> The main advantage of registering and divulging some personal information is that it helps the website tailor its service to your needs and let you know about special offers and promotions you might be interested in.

As we mentioned in Chapter 2, you will see a closed padlock, or some other similar security symbol, at the bottom of your web browser window when you are in secure mode. You should also see the web address changed to begin **https://** instead of the usual **http://**. When you're not in secure mode, the padlock will be open and the address will revert to its normal state.

Encrypting data takes a lot of computer resources and can slow things down considerably on the web, so when you're just browsing a website you don't want to be in secure mode unless you have to. You only need security when you're about to send personal and sensitive information across the net. So online retailers will often give you the option of switching between secure and insecure mode to help speed up your browsing experience.

It's safer paying by credit card

Despite the security fears about using credit cards online, they actually give you *more* protection, not less. This is because Section 75 of the Consumer Credit Act 1974 states that you have an equal claim against the card issuer if the retailer goes bust or fails to deliver the goods in a satisfactory condition. Providing the value of the transaction is worth at least £100 and not more than £30,000 per item, you're covered. This applies even if you've only used the card to pay a deposit. You can find more information about this on the Office of Fair Trading's website (*see page 42 for the address*). NB: You don't have this protection if you pay using debit or charge cards.

> **WARNING**
>
> *Never buy from a retailer that doesn't offer secure online payments.*

How can I trust an online retailer?

It is very important to check out a retailer's credentials before you buy from it. If you've never heard of the company you need to be extra careful, especially if it's a foreign site. On the web it is very easy for fraudsters to set themselves up as legitimate businesses, then simply take your credit card details and scarper without delivering the goods you ordered. After all, creating a website is a lot easier than setting up a false shop front on the high street.

As well as being on guard against possible fraudsters, you need to be wary of sites that do not maintain high standards when it comes to customer service and security. How do you know that the retailer will process your order accurately and on time? How do you know that your personal details are safe from prying eyes, whether inside or outside the company? The brutal truth is that you don't. You have to satisfy yourself about the genuineness and reliability of websites, and this means checking them out and using your common sense.

Follow these rules and you should be safe:

1. Never give your plastic card or personal details over the net except via a secure server.

2. Never write down or disclose passwords, log-in names or Personal Identification Numbers (PINs).

3. Stick to well-known, well-regarded websites if possible. Ask friends for recommendations.

4. If you've never heard of a website and you're unsure about it, look for physical address and telephone contact details. Test them to establish that the business really exists. Ask your friends if they've heard of it. If you have any remaining doubts, don't deal with them.

5. Also check that the web address is exactly right. Fraudsters can sometimes set up virtual copies of well-known brand-name websites. A dot here and a hyphen there can make all the difference. And bear in mind that a **.co.uk** or **.uk** ending doesn't necessarily mean that the site is based in the UK.

Sites such as Internet Fraud Watch (www.fraud.org) gives news on the latest net frauds and scams.

● Look for sites that have been given a 'kitemark' certificate by an accreditation scheme, such as TrustUK, VeriSign, Which? WebTrader, TrustE, BBBOnLine, and JIPDEC (*see page 31 for more details*).

● If a web retailer says it belongs to a trade association, check that it really does and find out whether the association operates a code of conduct and any kind of arbitration service should you need to make a complaint.

● Look for sites that send you an e-mail confirming your order and giving you a unique order number that you can use to track the progress of your purchase. Make sure you keep these e-mails as proof of purchase and for reference if you need to contact the retailer.

● Ask what delivery guarantees the retailer gives and what its returns policy is. If it is a UK site you're covered by normal consumer law (*see page 33*) and entitled to a full refund if goods are faulty or not as advertised. Be extra vigilant when ordering from abroad because UK law doesn't apply.

● If a website is offering something that looks too good to be true, it probably is. Treat with extreme caution. For news on the latest net frauds and scams try sites such as **Internet Fraud Watch** (www.fraud.org) and **Internet Scambusters** (www.scambusters.com).

● Use a credit card to pay online. The card issuer is obliged to refund you under Section 75 of the Consumer Credit Act if the goods fail to arrive or are damaged (for purchases between £100 and £30,000). There is still a debate within the industry as to whether this law applies to foreign transactions. The Office of Fair Trading thinks it does, the card issuers disagree. At the moment though, they will refund you, but only on a voluntary basis.

'Kitemarks' for websites

Now it's all very well giving all the advice listed above. But for most of us, time is a precious commodity. We don't really want the hassle of having to check out every website before we buy anything. So the kind of 'kitemark' schemes mentioned above, that assess websites for authenticity, security, and responsibility in the handling of personal details, are very welcome.

Some schemes also go further and look at the sites' returns policies and all-round quality of customer service. The only problem is, there are several of them, and this is just confusing for online shoppers. What we really need is a single, global standard, but we're some way off from that at the moment.

In the US, as ever, they're a little ahead of the game. Companies like VeriSign, Digisign, Cybertrust, Entrust, TrustE and P3P (Privacy Preferences Project) all offer versions of the same kind of 'standards' guarantee. There is a bias towards technical proficiency rather than an assessment of all-round customer service, though.

We are beginning to catch up in the UK. The Consumers' Association got the ball rolling with its **Which? WebTrader** scheme – probably the most successful 'code of practice' scheme for online shopping sites so far. To display the WebTrader logo on their sites, online retailers have to conform to a number of stringent 'good practices', such as displaying total prices (including delivery) clearly, agreeing a delivery date with shoppers and offering a refund if this isn't met. The Consumers' Association regulates WebTrader sites itself and promises removal and 'humiliation' for websites that fail to keep up the standards.

TIP

Look for the sites that carry the following logos, guaranteeing a degree of reliability and services:

Webtrader

IMRG

TrustUK

Interactive Media in Retail Group (IMRG), an electronic commerce forum with over 400 members in 20 countries, operates a voluntary code of practice for its members. Those in compliance with the code can display the IMRG logo. IMRG also promises to follow up consumer complaints against any online retailer. You can see a list of companies that subscribed to IMRG's code of practice on its website (*see page 44*).

And now the Government and a whole host of trade associations, including the Confederation of British Industry and the Direct Marketing Association, have co-operated in developing TrustUK, the first national 'kitemark' or 'hallmark' scheme, aimed at giving online shoppers complete confidence in retailer sites bearing the TrustUK logo. In time, this should make all other UK schemes redundant, since it has the backing of most of the industry.

Companies wanting accreditation have to ensure their advertising and contracts are fair and balanced, that shopping systems are secure, and that a privacy code of practice is clearly available. At the time of writing, no websites had been accredited yet, but the system was scheduled to begin officially in May 2000.

TrustUK is a non-profit organization run by industry with the support and backing of Government. It will police the system itself and consider appeals from disgruntled shoppers who feel that a web retailer hasn't lived up to the code and hasn't handled their complaints properly.

Your rights under the law

A s far as UK law and the regulators are concerned, there's no difference between shopping online and shopping by mail order or in the high street. UK consumer protection law applies equally well. These state that goods must be:

● **as described on the website**

● **of satisfactory quality**

● **fit for their purpose.**

This is why it's important to make records of your transactions. Print off web pages containing product particulars so you have something to refer to when the product arrives. Keep any e-mails, too. If you're not happy, you must have evidence to show that the retailer was in breach of the law as summarized above. If a retailer had pointed out a defect, say, and you hadn't noticed the warning on the website, you would forfeit your right to compensation.

These consumer rights also apply to goods in sales. The retailer is obliged to offer you a full refund if the product doesn't come up to scratch.

Of course, if you just change your mind after pressing the 'Buy Now!' button, or you decide you don't like your purchase when it arrives, you'll have a hard time getting your money back. Having said that, many retailers do operate a 'good will' policy, and offer refunds or exchanges even when they don't have to under the law. It's a good idea to find out whether the online retailer does operate such a policy before you buy online. Some shoppers may feel that it's worth paying a little extra for something at a particular site they know won't cause a fuss if they need to return it for whatever reason. Members of the Direct Marketing Association allow customers to return goods within seven days (*see page 44*).

> **TIP**
>
> *It's important to make records of your transactions.*

If you're not happy ...

The same consumer principles apply to online shopping as apply to ordinary shopping. If the goods you buy online are faulty, or not what you thought you ordered, you must tell the retailer as soon as possible. A long delay can work in the retailer's favour if a dispute arises – it can be interpreted as acceptance on your part. It also gives weight to the retailer's potential argument that you must have damaged the item yourself and you just want to get your money back unfairly. Prompt action gives slippery retailers far less room for manoeuvre.

One of the many advantages of e-mail is that you can complain very quickly. It's also easy to keep copies of correspondence, unlike telephone calls. Keeping receipts is obviously a good idea also.

Don't be put off if a retailer tries to escape its obligations. It can't just pass the buck and blame the manufacturer. If the goods come with a manufacturer's guarantee, though, it may be sensible to send off the registration card. Sometimes you get extra protection.

You are normally obliged to accept a retailer's offer to mend the goods if they are faulty, but you're under no pressure to accept them if the repairs don't work. You can still ask for compensation, although technically you're thought to have 'accepted' the goods by then. And bear in mind that just because goods are in a sale, it doesn't mean the retailer is not responsible if they turn out to be dodgy. You should expect some wear and tear on second-hand goods, but they should still comply with the main principles listed above.

Who to complain to ...

If you don't get anywhere with the retailer and you're still dissatisfied, there are a number of bodies you can complain to. A list of useful web addresses is given on page 42. The relevant organization will depend largely on the type of complaint.

35

For example, the retailer may belong to a trade association that has a code of practice for its members. If the web company is in breach of the code the association should take up the case on your behalf. Some associations operate low-cost arbitration services to sort out disputes between customers and their members. The existence of a code of practice also helps other bodies judge whether the member company has been acting unfairly or unlawfully.

Alternatively you could seek advice from a **Citizens Advice Bureau** or from **Trading Standards** departments. Trading standards departments have powers to investigate complaints about false or misleading descriptions or prices, and the safety of consumer goods (except in Northern Ireland). They will often advise on everyday shopping problems and are usually all too aware of unreliable or troublesome retailers. If you're not sure about a particular website, it may be an idea to ring a trading standards office first, to see if they've had any complaints about it.

You can also seek the advice of a solicitor – some working in law centres or advice agencies will offer advice for free. Your local Citizens Advice Bureau can help you find a low-cost or free solicitor. As a last resort, you could take the retailer to court, although this can be expensive and time-consuming.

If your complaint is about the way something is being advertised on the web, go to the **Advertising Standards Authority**. The ASA is responsible for enforcing British Codes of Advertising and Sales Promotion, whether the ads are on the TV, in newspapers or on the net. Ads must be legal, decent, honest and truthful.

The ASA code states that you are entitled to a full refund if you return the goods within seven days of receiving them. And you don't have to pay if they've taken so long to arrive that you don't want them any more. The standard time limit for deliveries is 30 days.

E-mail is often used for direct marketing purposes and many of the companies that advertise this way belong to the **Direct Marketing Association**. The DMA has an independent adjudication service to help in disputes between customers and member firms. It also offers a useful e-mail privacy protection service (*see* **Protecting your privacy**, *page 38*).

Although this doesn't strictly apply in a guide about shopping, if your complaint is anything to do with financial services, the **Financial Services Authority**, the newly empowered single regulator for the financial services industry, runs an ombudsman scheme to investigate complaints on behalf of consumers.

Buying from individuals

When you buy something from a private individual, through a classified ads website, for example, you're much less protected. The old rule – 'caveat emptor' – applies. But the goods still must be 'as described'. So if someone is selling a car and describes it as 'in pristine condition' and you discover that it's a rust-bucket, you're entitled to a refund. In practice, this can be difficult to enforce. For this reason, some unscrupulous retailers pose as private sellers to flog off substandard goods in a less regulated environment.

> **WARNING**
>
> *When you buy something from a private individual, through a classified ads website, for example, you're much less protected.*

Looking to the future

The transnational nature of the net is forcing domestic governments to harmonize consumer legislation, especially in the European Union, where integration has been going on for years. The main piece of legislation that should help online shoppers is the European Distance Selling Directive. It standardizes the information that retailers have to provide, such as your rights if you decide not to go ahead with the purchase or contract. It requires that delivery costs and any other charges must be displayed clearly and so on. This new law is meant to be implemented in all EU member states by 4 June 2000.

Protecting your privacy

Privacy is becoming more of an issue than credit card security. When you register at a website retailers can glean a lot of information about you that an ordinary bricks-and-mortar shop wouldn't find out. Even when you don't register and you surf from site to site, you leave a trail behind you. For example, websites know what sections of their site you clicked on, what you were interested in, and what web browser you use.

> ### FACT
>
> *The transnational nature of the net is forcing domestic governments to harmonize consumer legislation, especially in the European Union.*

Understandably, this has caused a lot of concern amongst net users. Firstly, some people don't like the idea of websites knowing anything about their surfing habits and tastes, and secondly, there's concern over what websites do with all the information they've acquired. Marketing companies are always interested in finding out as much about consumers as possible so that they can target advertising more effectively. They are prepared to pay handsomely for this kind of information and websites are only too happy to sell it to them.

At least, that was the way it used to be. With all the attention paid to privacy, things have started to improve and websites have begun to make a feature of not forwarding personal details to third parties. Reputable sites will draw your attention to their 'Privacy Statement' or 'Privacy Policy'. This will tell you what the company intends to do with the information it gathers about you and what steps it takes to protect this information from unauthorized access. Always read these statements if you're concerned about protecting your privacy online.

Again, retailers know that this is a major concern for online shoppers and they want to bend over backwards to alleviate any fears consumers have. Under the law, you now have to be given the option either to give or to withdraw your consent for personal information to be shared with other companies, even within the same group.

This usually involves ticking a box when you register on a website. But make sure you look carefully at the way such opt-outs are worded. Some ask you to tick the box if you don't want your personal details divulged, others assume that you don't at the outset. Any company that sells on details of an enquiry or transaction without your consent or knowledge could be in breach of UK and EU law.

TIP

Reputable sites will draw your attention to their 'Privacy Statement' or 'Privacy Policy'. This will tell you what the company intends to do with the information it gathers about you and what steps it takes to protect this information from unauthorized access.

So be careful only to divulge information you are happy to give out. If it's not strictly necessary for a website to know your age, sex and salary-bracket, say, don't fill in those sections of the registration form. If the site insists, don't use it. We've seen above how you should be careful when entering payment card details, and the same level of caution should apply to personal details.

Unwanted e-mail

If you aren't careful about who you give your details away to you may find your e-mail box swamped with unwanted e-mails offering you services you didn't ask for and don't need. This kind of e-mail is known as spam. Companies can buy huge lists of e-mail addresses that have been gleaned from websites, bulletin board discussions groups, usenet forums and other e-mails. They can then send thousands and thousands of e-mails with a few clicks of a mouse and reach far more people that they could ever have dreamed of before, at a fraction of the cost.

Although most of these messages may be genuine adverts, others may be completely bogus schemes, competitions and special offers perpetrated by fraudsters with easy access to your in-box. As we've said before, if an offer looks too good to be true, it probably is. And always be wary of any scheme that insists you act quickly or asks you to send money in advance.

You can usually tell a spam mail if your e-mail address doesn't appear in the 'To:' box of the header section. Your address will have been placed in the 'Blind Carbon Copy' (Bcc) box. The sender's address may also be fictitious. The best thing to do is not to respond at all. Without a response the sender has no evidence that your address is still 'live'. People frequently change e-mail address and lists aren't always up-to-date. If you just delete such messages immediately the sender may eventually give up.

But if you're being plagued by such messages, you could complain to your internet service provider (ISP). Some ISPs have successfully banned known spam mailers from using their servers. And in the latest versions of e-mail programs there are security features that allow you to filter out unwanted messages. These are far from perfect, but they are a step in the right direction.

The content of spam e-mails is covered by the British Codes of Advertising and Sales Promotion, the Control of Misleading Advertisements Regulations 1988, and the Trade Descriptions Act 1968. Complain to the relevant body if the claims being made in such e-mails clearly contradict any of these codes and laws.

The Direct Marketing Association also runs a useful e-mail preference service. You can register your e-mail address on the site if you don't wish to

> **TIP**
>
> *If you receive unsolicited mail (spam), the best thing to do is not to respond at all. Without a response the sender has no evidence that your address is still 'live'.*

receive unsolicited e-mails from any of its members. As most direct marketing companies are members of the DMA, this is a pretty comprehensive service.

Once you've registered on the site (*see page 44 for web address*), all DMA members have to delete your address from their mail lists. The EU's Distance Selling Directive will also require that e-mails for distance selling purposes should only be used when there is no clear objection from the consumer. This means that you will have the chance to choose not to receive unsolicited e-mails and have your choice respected.

If spam continues to be a problem, you may also be able to get help from the Data Protection Registrar, who polices the use of personal data held on computers. The only snag is that the Registrar's powers are limited to the UK, so foreign-sourced e-mails are out of bounds.

Offensive material
The Internet Watch Foundation (IWF) is a self-regulation body funded by the UK internet industry as an initiative supported by the Department of Trade & Industry, the Home Office and UK police forces. It was established to fulfil an independent role in receiving and processing complaints about child pornography and other illegal material on the internet.

The IWF operates a hotline service for internet users to report potentially illegal material. IWF assesses all the material reported and, where appropriate, advises UK internet service providers to remove it and passes information to the police.

Any UK resident can contact the IWF 24 hours a day to let them know about material on the internet which they consider to be potentially harmful. The IWF can be contacted by phone (on 08456 00 88 44 – local-rate calls), by e-mail **report@internetwatch.org.uk** or via their website at http://www.iwf.org.uk.

Useful web addresses

Office of Fair Trading	**www.oft.gov.uk/html/shopping**
Trading Standards Office	**www.tradingstandards.gov.uk**
Northern Ireland	
Trading Standards	**www.tssni.gov.uk/ conspubs.htm**
National Association of	
Citizens Advice Bureaux	**www.nacab.org.uk**

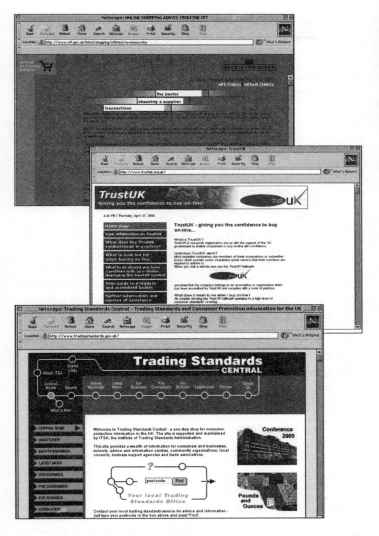

Some useful web addresses: the Office of Fair Trading (www.oft.gov.uk/html/ shopping, top); TrustUK (www.trustuk.org.uk, centre); Trading Standards Office (www.tradingstandards.gov.uk, bottom).

Advertising Standards Authority	www.asa.org.uk
Direct Marketing Association	www.dma.org.uk
Directory of British and Irish Ombudsmen	www.intervid.co.uk/bioa
Data Protection Registrar	www.dpr.gov.uk
E-mail Preference Service	www.e-mps.org/en
TrustUK	www.trustuk.org.uk
Which? WebTrader Scheme	www.which.net/ webtrader/index.html
Interactive Media in Retail Group	www.imrg.org

Chapter 4

Useful Starting Points

There are thousands and thousands of online retailers out there on the web, all clamouring for your attention. More are going online every day. The net is becoming a very big and crowded marketplace and it's easy to get lost. So how do you know which sites are good, reliable and value for money? Well, you read our site guide in Chapter 8, of course, but there are also a number of good jumping-off points to begin with and services that can help make shopping online easier and more productive.

In this chapter we look at such places – shopping mall sites and shop directories – and give you tools to find what you want at the best price. Shopping clubs that negotiate discounts for members are also becoming popular, and there are points schemes around that reward you for visiting certain sites. Canny use of all of these can save you time and money.

In fact, in my view, this chapter is more important than Chapter 8, which is basically a list of good retail websites. As online shopping progresses and becomes more sophisticated, we won't bother going direct to retailer sites unless we're sure that they, and they alone, can provide what we want at a price we're happy with. Our first port of call will be the kind of sites described below.

Shopping portals, directories and price comparison engines

If you're not sure what you want to buy and you just fancy browsing, try a shopping-mall style portal, directory or price comparison engine for starters. Virtual shopping malls attempt to recreate the feel of a shopping centre with a pictorial approach. You usually see images of shop fronts bearing the logos of the retailers. If you click on one of these you go through to the retailer's website.

Shopping directories tend to be less ornamental but probably more use, providing links to hundreds of other retail sites. They often provide other services, too, such as general security advice, shopping guides, and independent assessments of the sites on their lists. They are becoming more sophisticated in the quality of advice they give consumers. Although there are stand-alone services around, more and more ISPs are incorporating shopping sections in their portal websites. Some ISPs and other service providers offer an added layer of security for their members by vetting retailers before listing them. They can often negotiate discounts on behalf of their members, too.

Some directories and shopping portals incorporate price comparison engines or agents into their websites. With these you enter the product you're looking for and the engine scans all the retailers on its list looking for the cheapest price. Some include the cost of delivery in the price comparison, although none are sophisticated enough yet to work out the impact of import taxes as well. They are also usually restricted to a few categories, such as books, CDs, videos, DVDs, computer games and software.

In time the number of categories and the number of retailers within each category will grow and price comparison engines will become one of the most important services on the net. Anything that makes it easier to shop around for online bargains has got to be a winner. You won't need to go direct to retailers' websites any more. Price comparison agents also force retailers to become more competitive since any overpriced goods just won't show up in searches. This will inevitably lead to lower prices and may even lead to a few store closures as well.

General shopping sites seem to be springing up all over the place. Here's a selection of the most useful sites around, including shopping portals and price comparison engines.

ShopSmart –
www.shopsmart.com

ShopSmart – formerly ShopGuide – is a new player in the online shopping world and it is certainly making a big splash, spending millions on a high-profile TV advertising campaign and buying up other directory sites. For example, it has snapped up Enterprise City, the excellent shopping directory, and so offers links to 1,500 online retailers, all of which have been reviewed using a star rating.

When you click on one of its categories or 'Departments' as it likes to call them, the sites are ranked according to their ratings. There is also a price comparison engine covering books, music CDs, DVDs and videos. The site obviously intends to become a one-stop shop and is well on the way to

The ShopSmart site, a new player in the online shopping world, is well on the way to becoming a one-stop shop.

becoming one. You can even download a small program that will incorporate a ShopSmart button into your Internet Explorer browser (version IE5 only).

Interactive Media in Retail Group (IMRG) –
www.imrg.org

IMRG is an industry association that also carries out regular independent 'mystery shopper' exercises, reviewing and rating hundreds of online retailers. It runs its own 'hallmark' scheme to give consumers confidence and has an excellent directory of around 3,000 non-US retail websites. You can search for shops by category or keyword.

IMRG has also devised its own 'hotel-guide'-style symbols to indicate what level of security the shops offer, what payment methods they accept, and how far they will deliver. It also tells you whether the site has been awarded a quality 'kitemark' by a trusted organization. You can access any site

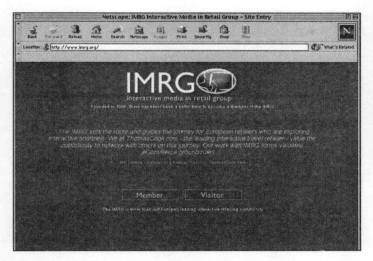

IMRG carries out regular independent 'mystery shopper' exercises, reviewing and rating hundreds of online retailers.

reviews IMRG has carried out. It has also launched a free ISP service and there is an icon that can be downloaded on to your desktop that will take you straight through to the shopping directory once you click on it. If it added a price comparison engine to its directory it would be even better.

MyTaxi – www.mytaxi.co.uk

MyTaxi started out as a price comparison agent with global ambitions. It has since scaled back somewhat to settle for a more basic shopping directory site with some price comparison tools and other innovative features. Retailers can advertise special deals on the Taxi home page to entice shoppers to their sites, and registered members can receive discounts on some goods. You can also tailor the page so that just your favourite stores are featured – it has over 1,400 listed. You will then see adverts from them promoting their latest special offers. The only drawback with the site is that it

MyTaxi is a shopping directory site with some price comparison tools. It allows you to tailor the page so that just your favourite stores are featured.

is quite scatty in its design and it lacks a bit of focus. It is also still fairly US orientated, but worth a look all the same.

BTSpree – www.btspree.co.uk

BTSpree was launched by British Telecom and eBusiness as another one-stop shop service, incorporating a shopping directory and price comparison services. BTSpree's strength is clearly its search engine, powered by Inktomi. It lets you search by product, by manufacturer, by store or by price. You can also choose whether to search in the UK, the US, or globally. You don't have to register to use it. The site features special offers from retailers as well as general shopping tips and guides. The number of retailers is fairly limited compared to other shopping directories, but growing fast.

ValueMad – www.valuemad.com

Founded by grocery chain ASDA, ValueMad is one of those sites that offers price comparison engines and a directory of

*Two other sites offering price comparison services: BTSpree
(www.btspree.co.uk, top) and ValueMad (www.valuemad.com, bottom).*

If you shop at Egg's shopping portal using the Egg credit card you get 2% cashback on goods bought from retailers in its directory.

shops that it has approved for security, value for money, and reliability. It gives each site marks out of ten and provides 'hotel-guide'-style symbols telling you more about delivery costs and whether it accepts telephone orders. It also tells you if the retailer is affiliated to the *Which?* WebTrader scheme (*see page 64*).

UKPlus – www.ukplus.co.uk

This search directory has a useful shopping section and, as its name suggests, it sticks to hundreds of UK sites only. There's also a 'Best Buy' section and price comparisons, plus a useful car finder tool.

Egg Shopping – http://shopping.egg.com

An internet banking website may seem an odd place for a shopping portal, but if you use Egg's credit card you get 2% cashback on goods bought from retailers in its directory.

Although it's a bit of a gimmick, Egg also promises to

If you can't find what you're looking for anywhere else, a 'catch-all' site such as UKShopping may prove useful.

reimburse anyone who is defrauded while shopping online using the Egg card (*see* **Safe Shopping**, *page 21*). Egg is being selective in its choice of retailers with over 100 to choose from, rather than thousands. It believes, rightly, that quality is better than quantity, preferring to make sure that its chosen retailers are safe, reliable and willing to offer special deals. It is keen to build up a sense of community by incorporating website reviews from shoppers, too.

UKShopping – http://ukshopping.com

An action-packed shopping directory aiming to be the most comprehensive for UK web retailers. It comes from the Special Reserve Discount Network, a specialist mail-order company that has a number of discount websites. It also offers a free net access package called Freeola. If you can't find what you're looking for anywhere else, a 'catch-all' site like this may prove useful.

Two other popular shopping directories: Bigsave (www.bigsave.com, above) and I Want To Shop (www.iwanttoshop.com, below)

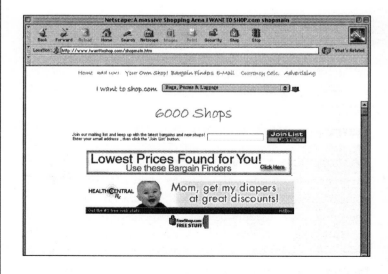

Bigsave – www.bigsave.com

This new discount online shopping centre offers 16 departments with over 7,000 products. It promises savings of up to 72% on well-known brand name goods. It is well organized and avoids that 'cheap' feeling you often get with discount retailers.

I Want To Shop – www.iwanttoshop.com

Another shopping directory that has been expanding rapidly. It now has over 6,000 shops on its site – a mix of UK and US – very stringently categorized to help you find what you're looking for. There are also links to US and European price comparison agents and other useful services, such as a currency converter.

Barclaysquare – www.barclaysquare.com

Barclaysquare was one of the UK's first virtual shopping malls, trying to recreate the look and feel of a conventional

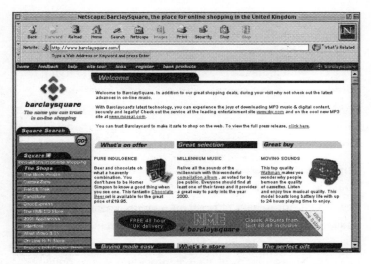

The Barclaysquare shopping directory has introduced some innovative features, such as interactive product selectors.

The Virgin Net ISP has opted for quality rather than quantity and vets its retailers before featuring them on the site.

shopping centre. Thankfully it has ditched this approach as being too fiddly and unnecessary. An over-reliance on graphics just makes for slower download times and frustrated shoppers. It now looks more like a conventional shopping directory with a limited selection of shops. But it is trying to introduce some innovative features, such as interactive product selectors. There's a What Video & TV section that allows you to set the parameters for the type of model you're looking for, and pictures of the recommended models appear.

Virgin Net – www.virgin.net

Virgin Net is an ISP that has adopted the same strategy as Egg, opting for quality rather than quantity and vetting its retailers before featuring them on the site. Retailers wanting a 'Virgin Recommends' tag have to agree to offer 5% cashback to Virgin Net members, as well as providing secure online ordering and delivery guarantees.

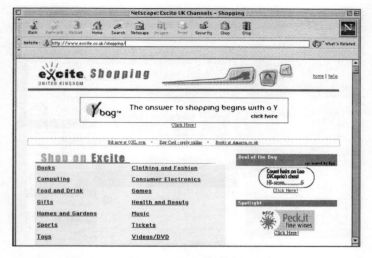

Most portal sites, including Excite, now incorporate shopping directories.

Some other ISPs and portals with shopping sections....

Yahoo UK	http://uk.shopping.yahoo.com
Freeserve	www.freeserve.net/shopping
Excite	www.excite.co.uk/shopping
Microsoft Network	www.msn.co.uk
LineOne	www.lineone.net
Zoom	www.zoom.co.uk
UK Max	www.ukmax.com/shopping

Dedicated price comparison agents

Shopgenie – www.shopgenie.com

This price comparison service makes great play of the fact that it checks the prices listed by all the retailers in real time, ensuring that the very latest prices are quoted. It vets the

The LineOne ISP also has a shopping section.

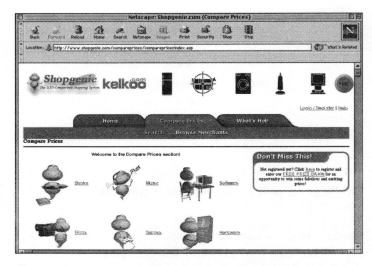

This price comparison service Shopgenie checks the prices listed by all the retailers in real time, ensuring that the very latest prices are quoted.

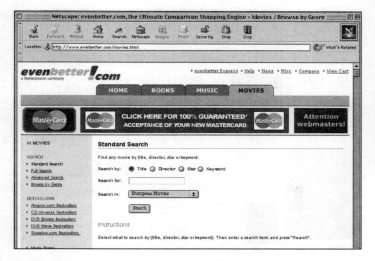

Evenbetter.com takes delivery costs into account when ranking prices and can display the prices in whichever currency you choose.

retailers in its directory, too. As with most other price comparison services, it covers books, music, films, games, software and hardware. It has recently added a wine price comparison service, too. As we went to press, Shopgenie was in the process of merging with Kelkoo.com, a European shopping directory, and will eventually take its name as well.

Evenbetter.com – www.evenbetter.com

This excellent books, CDs and films comparison engine was formerly called DealPilot. The best things about Evenbetter.com are the way it takes delivery costs into account when ranking the prices and its ability to display the prices in a currency of your choice, even if the sites are foreign. If only it could work out the effect of import taxes, too, it would be perfect.

BookBrain – www.bookbrain.co.uk

Even more focused than DealPilot, BookBrain sticks to books and does its job extremely well as a result. You can search by

BookBrain allows you to search for books by author, title, publisher or ISBN for books in the inventories of 14 UK online bookshops.

author, title, publisher or ISBN for books in the inventories of 14 UK online bookshops, making it nigh impossible for you to miss what you're looking for.

The results of your search are ranked by price, including delivery charges. There's also information on typical availability and delivery times.

Comparing prices abroad...

If you want to see what's available in the US, there are a number of price comparison engines over there, many far more sophisticated in their breadth and depth than the UK versions. The best I've come across are:

BottomDollar	**www.bottomdollar.com**
MySimon	**www.mysimon.com**
PriceScan	**www.pricescan.com**
Shopper.com	**www.shopper.com**
Virtual Outlet	**http://vo.infospace.com**

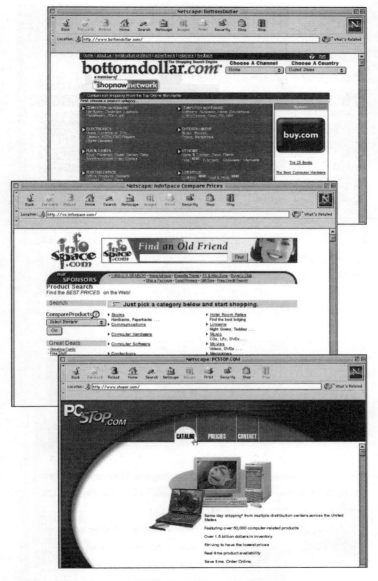

If you want to shop in the US, use a price comparison engine such as BottomDollar (top), Virtual Outlet (centre) or Shopper.com (bottom).

Shopping clubs

Blue Carrots — www.bluecarrots.com

This is a new online shopping concept based on the notion that members own the company and are rewarded with shares so long as they visit the site at least once a week. Its directory contains over 1,000 shops, but CarrotClub members can receive discounts of up to 15% on over a million products from 90 partner retailers. You can use Blue Carrots as your ISP and set up a web-based Carrot e-mail address. In fact you only qualify for the discounts if you click through to the partner retailer from the Blue Carrots site and you give a Carrot e-mail address. The whole concept revolves around loyalty to the club. For it to work, you have to love it so much you visit the site on a regular basis. There are other services on the site, such as football scores and news stories, but some people will find the enforced loyalty too restrictive.

Blue Carrots is a new online shopping concept based on the idea that members own the company and are rewarded with shares.

Let'sBuyIt – www.letsbuyit.com

This is a pan-European brand intended to bring collective
bargaining power to internet shopping. The idea is that
if lots of people want the same product, the retailer will
be able to offer it at a lower price. It calls these joint
purchases 'co-buys'. The more people join a co-buy, the
lower the price drops. There is a target 'best price' and a
'current price' dependent upon how many people have
joined the co-buy. Each co-buy has a time-limit placed
upon it – a few weeks normally – much like an online
auction. You can choose to buy only at the 'best price' or at
the current price. Given that it's in your interest to get as
many other people interested as possible, you can tip off
friends by e-mail.

LetsBuyIt sources direct from manufacturers, thus
cutting out many of the overheads associated with
conventional buying in the high street. Once you've joined

*Let'sBuyIt is a pan-European brand intended to bring collective bargaining
power to internet shopping. The idea is that if lots of people want the same
product, the retailer will be able to offer it at a lower price.*

Which? Online provides in-depth consumer reports as well as discounts on goods sold by a number of Which? retail partners.

a co-buy, you can't back out, but you can return the product within 30 days of receiving it and get a full refund. There are disadvantages with this concept, not least the need to wait for others to join your co-buy, and the fact that you're restricted to what other people want to buy as well. But for popular products that have high recommended retail prices, the potential bargains are impressive.

Which? Online – www.which.net

If you subscribe to *Which?* **Online**, not only do you get access to all *Which?* Magazine's in-depth consumer reports, but you also receive discounts on goods sold by a number of *Which?* retail partners. You can buy white goods, home appliances, electronics and cameras, as well as CDs, books and films. All its partners meet its WebTrader 'kitemark' standards for security and efficiency.

Loyalty schemes

The problem with the web these days is that there are just so many sites to visit. Online retailers trying to attract custom must feel like they're shouting to be heard in the middle of a very large and crowded bazaar. Loyalty points schemes are one way they can attract customers, either operating them at their own sites, much like supermarket loyalty cards, or subscribing to an externally run points scheme.

With retailer-run schemes the more you spend the more points you earn. You can then redeem them against products once you've built up a sufficient store. Shopping portal **Zoom** (**www.zoom.co.uk**) runs just such a scheme.

With externally run schemes surfers can pick up points in a number of ways. For example, you can often pick up points just as a reward for visiting a particular site. Sometimes, bonus points will be hidden somewhere on the site, encouraging surfers to peruse the entire site and perhaps buy a product or click on some of the banner adverts. Sometimes you may be offered points as an incentive to take part in a market research survey. You can redeem the points at participating retailers' websites.

The most successful points scheme so far is **beenz.com** (**www.beenz.com**), which claims to be the net's first currency. Despite the scheme's undoubted success – over a million users worldwide had collected and spent beenz after just one year of operation – it is far from becoming a currency in its own right. After all, more than 10 million people collect points using Tesco's ClubCard but we'd hardly call supermarket loyalty points a currency, neither do we consider AirMiles to be a currency.

Beenz.com sells beenz – unique electronic tokens – to retailers for one cent per bean. It is then up to the retailer to

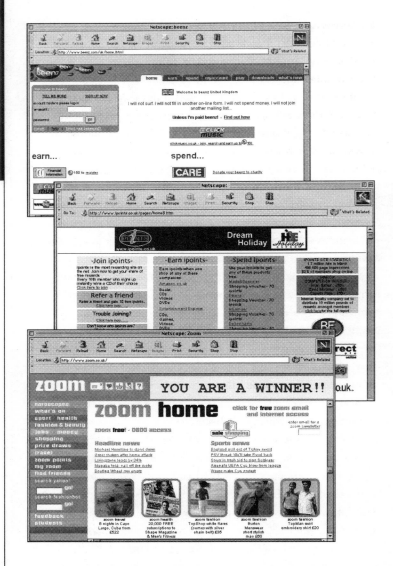

Some retailers subscribe to points schemes such as those run by beenz.com (www.beenz.com, top) or i-points (www.ipoints.co.uk, centre), while some shopping portals such as Zoom (www.zoom.co.uk, bottom) have their own loyalty schemes.

decide what to do with them and how much they are worth. So 6,000 beenz on one site might be worth a £20 discount, on another, £30. It depends how desperate the retailer is to get your custom.

Beenz.com controls the issue and redemption of beenz on its central database. You can view your beenz tally and transaction history online at any time by keying in your password. The system is admirably simple, but its success relies on its ability to build enough momentum so that the majority of retailers offer beenz. Otherwise it's difficult to believe too many shoppers are going to go out of their way to collect beenz from sites they might not otherwise visit to redeem them against products they would not ordinarily want to buy.

Another similar scheme that may not have the same marketing panache, is **i-points (www.ipoints.co.uk)**, which restricts itself to UK retail partners. One i-point is typically worth between 4p and 8p, depending on the retailer.

Chapter 5

Online Auctions

Online auctions have been one of the surprise successes of the net. In fact auction services, such as **eBay** (**www.ebay.com**), have been some of the very few net companies to make a profit. Online auctions combine the thrill of the chase with interactivity only usually associated with conventional shopping. People shop at online auctions in the hope of finding a bargain, or to find what they can't get hold of elsewhere. It reintroduces an entertainment element into online shopping. It is an excellent way for companies to sell off stock that has proved difficult to shift by other means, and for individuals to buy and sell items that might not be available in the shops.

It seems that people are auctioning everything these days, from airline tickets to bicycles, fine wines to Beanie Babies. But it is the world of art and collectibles that has most naturally and successfully moved online. After all, an auction is the fairest way to establish the value of a work of art, since it has no fixed value in the same way a manufactured product like a washing machine does. And the biggest growth area is proving to be person-to-person auctions – a step up from classified adverts.

Auction services such as eBay have been some of the very few net companies to make a profit.

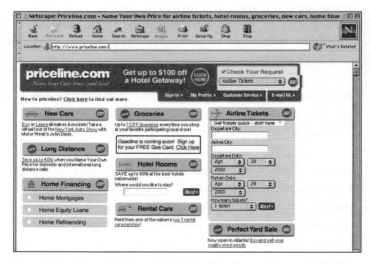

You can use a service such as Priceline.com to post a message online saying what you want and how much you are prepared to pay for it — a sort of reverse auction.

The net is perfectly suited to handling auction bidding, since it provides a single electronic platform for buyers who can be spread across the globe. It opens up new opportunities for people who may previously have been restricted to their local auctions. And it can handle the bidding for you even if you're not at your computer.

Soon we're going to see an extension of the auction principle that will give online shoppers even more power. The so-called reverse auction, whereby surfers post a message online saying what they want and how much they are prepared to pay for it, is already a reality in the US through services such as **Priceline.com** (**www.priceline.com**). This reverses the usual auction relationship since it is now the product or service providers who are competing with each other to pick up business. This kind of auction could have a massive impact.

Just imagine how prices would fall if people bought their cars this way, for example. You could have manufacturers competing for your business online, and dealerships cutting their commissions to offer you a deal. We're a few years off this at the moment, but it is coming.

How do online auctions work?

Registration

Most online auctions work in much the same way. First you have to register, which means filling in an online questionnaire, giving personal contact details, and maybe a credit card number. Remember that you should only submit credit details via a secure server that encrypts your details before they are sent across the web (*see* **Safe Shopping**, *page 21*). You have to set up a user name and password so that the auction can identify you. There's nothing to stop you registering with as many auctions as you like.

Registering usually involves agreeing to the auction site's terms and conditions. These may look dull and it is tempting to skip past them, but you should find out about the site's charges and its payment and delivery policies before bidding. Some sites leave it up to the buyer and seller to sort out payment and delivery. And different sellers will have their own preferences.

Browsing the lots

Auction sites tend to organize their lots – the items up for auction – by category. Some specialize in particular areas, such as art and collectibles or tickets for events, but most cover a range of categories. You can browse through looking for anything that might take your fancy, or go straight to the category you're interested in, whether computer games or stamps. Most sites have a search box to help you find what you're looking for.

The lots are often accompanied by a picture and a description, plus any related information that may be of use. Sometimes the pictures are very small and it can be difficult ascertaining the condition of the lot for sale. The better sites will provide an enlarged high-resolution version of the picture if you click on the thumbnail image.

TIP

Registering usually involves agreeing to the auction site's terms and conditions. These may look dull and it is tempting to skip past them, but you should find out about the site's charges and its payment and delivery policies before bidding. Some sites leave it up to the buyer and seller to sort out payment and delivery. And different sellers will have their own preferences.

Placing a bid

If you like what you see and you want to place a bid, you
have to log on, if you haven't already done so. This involves
typing in your user name and password. Depending on the
type of auction, you may then be allocated a unique number,
sometimes known as a paddle. This is to identify you. There
will usually be a box telling you the starting price for the lot,
whether there is a reserve price placed on it by the seller, the
latest bid, and the time remaining.

It may seem unfair, but you're not normally told what the
reserve price is. Don't assume that it's the starting price – it's
often higher than that. A low starting price is thought
necessary to get the ball rolling. You just have to keep on
bidding up until the lot shows the message 'The reserve has
been met' or something similar. Even if yours is the highest
bid, you won't win if the reserve hasn't been met.

When deciding how much to bid, the auction will usually
specify the agreed bid increment. This is variable. It can be
£1 for low-value items, but is usually around £10 or £20. You
can simply type in the next highest figure into the bid box
and press 'Submit', or the equivalent button. In a few minutes
your bid will then be shown on screen as the latest bid.
There's nothing to stop you making a *much* higher bid to
scare off rivals.

You should note that if
you win your bid, you
can't just change your
mind. You are
contractually obliged to
honour the transaction. If

> **TIP**
>
> *Even if yours is the highest bid, you won't
> win if the reserve hasn't been met.*

you have a change of heart and refuse to pay, the very least
the auction site could do is ban you from using the site again.

Automated bidding

Online auctions can take several weeks, so the last thing you want is to be tied to your computer checking to see if anyone has outbid you. Luckily most sites provide an automated bidding facility. All you do is enter your bid limit – the most you are prepared to pay for the lot – and then the site's computer will place bids on your behalf until your limit is reached. It will only go up to your limit if people keep outbidding you. This gives you freedom to do other things rather than slavishly watch your computer. If you're successful in your bidding, you'll be told by e-mail. If you don't fancy the automated bidding bit, some sites will just send you an e-mail when someone places a higher bid.

If you become addicted to auctions, placing bids on several sites, a service such as **BidStream** (**www.bidstream.com**) will help you keep a track of them all.

> ## WARNING
>
> *If you win your bid, you can't just change your mind. You are contractually obliged to honour the transaction. If you have a change of heart and refuse to pay, the very least the auction site could do is ban you from using the site again.*

Faster auctions

If you don't like all this hanging around, you can sometimes sort all the lots according to the time remaining. This gives you the option of choosing those lots that have only a few hours or minutes to go. This can inject a bit of excitement into what otherwise can be a fairly humdrum and long-winded process. It's also the quickest way to spot a potential bargain. If no-one has bid for a particular lot with only a few minutes to go, the chances are no-one will. You could nip in there at the last minute and snap it up. Bear in mind though that web auctions often reserve the right to

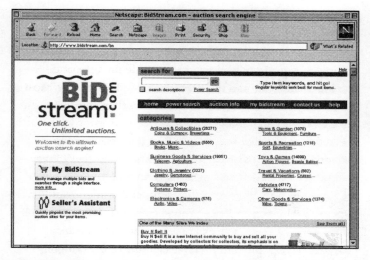

If you place bids on several sites, a service such as BidStream will help you keep a track of them all.

extend the auction if there is intense bidding going on at the death. This may seem like moving the goal-posts, but there we are.

Although most online auctions are spread out over a few days or weeks, they can also be live, with online bidders taking part in real auctions in an auction house. People in the room can be bidding against net surfers maybe several thousands miles away. This brings the excitement of the live auction room into bidders' homes. Some services even combine this with television for a true multimedia auction experience.

So far, such services are still in their infancy. We really need high-speed net connections to become the norm before live auctions take off in a big way. At the moment, the slowness and variability of net connections can introduce too many delays into what's supposed to be a fast-paced environment.

Delivery and charges

If you're successful in your bid, what happens next depends on the type of auction. For example, if the lot was sold by a company, it might have agreed to include the cost of delivery as part of the offer and take responsibility for delivery. With a person-to-person auction, it is often left up to both parties to decide how to take things forward.

As far as possible you should find out exactly what the delivery policy is and have a fair idea of the likely delivery cost before bidding. If the seller isn't willing to deliver, you may have to go and pick up the item, at considerable expense and inconvenience. You should also find out about other potential costs. For example, the auction site may charge a buyer's premium – typically 10% of the winning bid. There may also be local taxes and import taxes if you're buying from abroad. Most sites have useful 'Help' or 'Frequently Asked Questions' sections.

Placing your own auction advert

Most of the generalist auction sites allow people to place their own ads on the site for free, whereas some of the specialist art sites restrict this to affiliated dealers. How long such ads will remain free is in doubt. The established auction sites, such as **QXL** (**www.qxl.com**) intend to start charging for person-to-person ads.

Placing your own ad is simple enough. Once you've registered, you simply fill in an online application form giving details of the item you want to auction. Obviously the more arresting your description can be, the better. But avoid going over the top or you may end up in trouble with buyers and the auction site alike.

You can usually include a picture by attaching a graphics file along with your submission. You'll need a scanner to translate an ordinary photo into digital format or to take the

Auction sites such as QXL (www.qxl.com) intend to start charging for person-to-person ads.

picture using a digital camera. Look carefully at the site's guidelines if you want to do this, as there may be specific requirements for the size and type of file. Common graphics file formats are GIF, JPEG and Bitmap, but each site may have its own preferences. Once you've submitted your ad with a picture attached, be sure to check that the image has been properly loaded on the site. There have been cases of auction sites failing to do this correctly. As a picture considerably enhances your chances of attracting bidders, this part of the operation is crucial.

TIP

Once you've submitted your ad with a picture attached, be sure to check that the image has been properly loaded on the site. There have been cases of auction sites failing to do this correctly. As a picture considerably enhances your chances of attracting bidders, this part of the operation is crucial.

When filling out the form you're often given the chance to specify what payment methods you are prepared to accept and whether you expect the purchaser to pay for and arrange delivery. This all helps to avoid confusion later on.

Protecting yourself

When buying at auction you have fewer statutory rights than you do when buying from an ordinary online retailer. There is a grey area to do with the degree of responsibility the auction site will shoulder for the quality and authenticity of goods advertised on its site. By and large, 'buyer beware' operates.

Although public pressure has often led to the removal of auction items considered dangerous, illegal or offensive, this is still some way from the auctioneer accepting full responsibility for the items it does allow on its site.

At the time of writing, only **Sotheby's**, the art auction house, offered an authenticity guarantee for works advertised on its auction websites – **sothebys.com** and **sothebys.amazon.com**. At other sites, you're on your own. If you buy a fake, or something that turns out not to be as it was described in the auction ad, your powers of redress are limited.

If the seller is another retailer the terms of the contract will still be subject to the test of fairness set out in the Unfair Terms in Consumer Contracts Regulations 1994. But this

> **TIP**
>
> If you're remotely sceptical about the quality of the item being auctioned or the truthfulness of the description, don't touch it. You may be able to e-mail the seller direct and ask more questions about the item. In the end, you just have to trust people.

doesn't apply to private sellers. So look especially closely at the site's terms and conditions for any mention of guarantees and for information on what to do if you want to make a complaint.

Obviously an online auction company doesn't want to develop a reputation for harbouring fraudsters, liars and swindlers on its site, but there are limits to the amount of vetting it can do. Banning someone from advertising again is like closing the barn door after the horse has bolted, but it's the only real option open to the auction site.

If you're remotely sceptical about the quality of the item being auctioned or the truthfulness of the description, don't touch it. You may be able to e-mail the seller direct and ask more questions about the item. In the end, you just have to trust people.

Also bear in mind that online auction sites are not infallible. The systems they operate are complex and can go wrong from time to time. So it's important that you keep

A good online auction sites to visit is iCollector (www.icollector.com).

Art and collectibles auctions have made a natural and successful transition online.

records of the bidding process. For example, you should print off pages at crucial stages, such as when the the reserve has been met, and when you've been successful in your bid. The last thing you want is an e-mail from the auction site telling you you've bought something completely different at a price you cannot afford. This has happened before, so it's as well to have evidence to hand if you need to prove your case in a dispute. Also keep all e-mails you send to and receive from the auction site.

Online auction sites to visit

eBay	www.ebay.com or www.ebay.co.uk
iCollector	www.icollector.com
QXL	www.qxl.com
Yahoo! Auctions (UK)	http://uk.auctions.yahoo.com /uk
Amazon	www.amazon.com and www.amazon.co.uk
Loot	www.loot.com
Fired Up	www.firedup.com
Auction Hunter	www.auctionhunter.co.uk
Humpty	www.humpty.co.uk
eBid	www.ebid.co.uk
Priceline	www.priceline.com
Sotheby's.com	www.sothebys.com
Sotheby's-Amazon.com	www.sothebys.amazon.com
Artnet.com	www.artnet.com
GavelNet	www.gavelnet.com
The Auction Channel (live)	www.theauctionchannel.com
IbidLive (live)	www.ibidlive.com

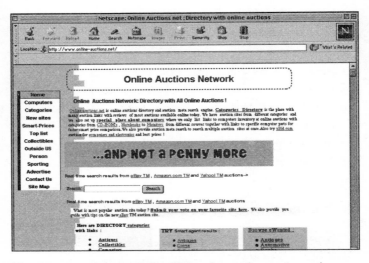

The auction search engine Online Auctions (www.online-auctions.net).

Auction search engines and directories

Bidstream	**www.bidstream.com**
Online Auctions	**www.online-auctions.net**
Bidfind	**www.bidfind.com**
Auction Guide	**www.auctionguide.com**

Shopping Abroad

One of the most amazing things about the net is its global reach. Retailers based thousands of miles away can come right to your computer screen. The net is becoming a worldwide marketplace giving surfers far wider choice and often better value as well. It also presents greater opportunities for local producers from Tibet to Turkey to market their goods and services to a whole new audience, cutting out a range of middlemen in the process. Ultimately this must be to our benefit.

But before we get carried away, bear in mind that the net is still largely a Western phenomenon, with half the world's online population based in the US and a significant proportion based in Europe. The other continents are only just beginning to catch up. In practice, the online shopping opportunities are limited in countries where the net is not widely available and telephone infrastructures are undeveloped.

So when we talk about shopping abroad we're really talking about shopping at US and European websites. And quite often you'll find that US websites won't even deliver abroad. For a mighty nation it can sometimes appear rather parochial.

So why shop abroad?

Quite simply, there are some massive bargains to be had. You can often buy CDs, books, and electronic goods far more cheaply from the US. As a very rough rule of thumb, when you see dollar prices you can pay the equivalent amount in sterling, despite the exchange rate differential. This means savings of up to 30%.

And thanks to the net, it's very easy to do. Many of the shopping portals, directories and price comparison engines mentioned in Chapter 4 (*see* **Useful Starting Points**, *page 45*) have links to foreign websites. In fact, if you've used a search engine to look for a particular product model, you can often be browsing around a site for several minutes before realizing that it's not UK-based. Even seeing all the prices in dollars doesn't always give the game away these days.

> **TIP**
>
> *As a very rough rule of thumb, when you see dollar prices you can pay the equivalent amount in sterling, despite the exchange rate differential.*

But, of course, there are risks and disadvantages:

● Goods can take weeks to arrive

● Your consumer rights may be severely limited (*see Safe Shopping, page 21*)

● If goods are faulty, getting them put right can be expensive and time-consuming

● Sometimes foreign specifications are not the same as in the UK e.g. power supplies, video formats – you may be paying less but for an inferior product or one that doesn't even work in the UK

● Delivery costs, local taxes, import duty and VAT can sometimes wipe out any savings you thought you'd made

● You may not know anything about the website you're dealing with

● Not all foreign websites will deliver to the UK.

How do I work out the total costs involved?

If you plan to shop abroad regularly, you'll need to learn how to do a few calculations to help you make proper comparisons with UK prices. Working out the sterling equivalent for the goods is easy enough. There have been around 1.6 dollars to the pound for a long time now. But if you want to be more accurate you could just open a new browser window and go to one of the many currency converters found on websites such as **UK-iNvest** (**www.uk-invest.com**) and **FT.com** (**www.ft.com**).

When you come to the virtual checkout the retail site will usually work out the delivery costs for you, although these charges are often not very clearly described on the site. Sometimes you have to go as far as entering your credit card details and delivery address before it will calculate the total charge. You can usually opt to pay more for express delivery if you'd rather receive your goods in a few days rather than a few weeks.

Depending on where you're buying from, there may be local taxes to pay. Then the fun really starts when the goods arrive at our shores. The rules governing import duties were obviously devised by a madman. Is there any real reason why duty should be 17% on ski boots, but only 2.7% on golf balls?

Websites such as UK-iNvest have currency converters that are useful if you intend to shop abroad.

Digital still cameras and computers are free from import duty, which is one reason why they can be much cheaper than in the UK. Books are also free from duty.

And there is no duty on goods ordered online and delivered into the UK from anywhere within the European Union. Also, digitized products, such as software and music clips, that you download are treated as services by Customs & Exercise (C&E) and so are free from duty. But you do have to pay VAT. And alcohol, tobacco and perfume always attract duty and VAT no matter where you've ordered from. Confused?

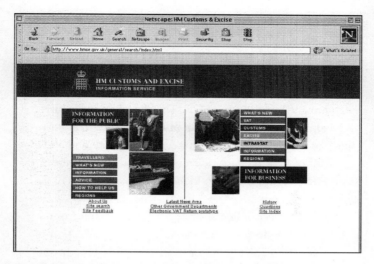

The Customs & Excise website has a section that gives duty rates for a number of commonly imported goods.

Customs & Excise, the government department responsible for all this, has a useful section on its website giving duty rates for a number of commonly imported goods. Point your browser at **www.hmce.gov.uk/general/search/index.htm** and bookmark the page. It isn't comprehensive by any means, so if the product you're considering importing isn't listed, you'll have to ring up C&E on 020 7202 4227 to ask for the relevant rate.

To find the amount of duty you have to pay you simply multiply the purchase price by the duty rate. You then add that amount on to the purchase price *before* applying Value Added Tax, usually at a rate of 17.5%. Art and antiques are subject to VAT at only 5%.

Just to make things even more complicated, you don't have to pay any import duty or VAT if the goods are worth less than £18 (£36 for gifts). Unfortunately this exemption doesn't apply to perfume, alcohol and tobacco. But it does mean that if you're quite careful about your purchasing frequency, you can buy CDs and other low-price goods very cheaply.

C&E knows what duty and VAT to apply because international packages must have a standard label giving the value and type of the goods. They'll only open your package if there's any doubt about the contents. The Post Office and other delivery companies collect duty and VAT on behalf of C&E when it delivers the goods – for a fee. Royal Mail charges £1.20, and Parcelforce charges £5.10 for standard deliveries.

But in practice, online shoppers who buy often from abroad could be forgiven for thinking that the collection of these taxes is completely hit or miss. I've often bought stuff from abroad worth considerably more than the £18 limit and yet it's been delivered without any extra charges being levied at all. The Consumers' Association has conducted shopping experiments and has found the same thing. Still, it would be unwise to factor in the inefficiency of our tax collection services when attempting to work out the total costs of importing goods from abroad.

Protecting yourself

A s we've pointed out above, there are potential pitfalls buying abroad. So here's a checklist of questions to ask before you flash the plastic:

Does the retailer deliver internationally?
This may seem a daft question to ask, but I've wasted a lot of time on websites trying to order stuff only to be told at the very last minute that it doesn't deliver internationally. US websites in particular often just assume that all their customers are domestic. I've even successfully placed an

order on a US website only to be told subsequently by e-mail that it couldn't process my order. That's a lot of wasted time. If there's no explicit information about international orders, you can usually tell when attempting to enter your delivery address details. If you're only given a selection of US states to choose from, the retailer probably doesn't deliver internationally. Some other websites make international customers complete the order over the phone.

Will the item work in the UK?

Check particularly that televisions, video games, computers, software, video recorders and video tapes are compatible in the UK. Ideally you should get the supplier to confirm this in writing before you buy.

Is it really a good deal?

Make sure you calculate the total cost (*see page 85*) to make sure you are comparing prices on a like-for-like basis. Also bear in mind that if there is a delay between the time you place the order and the time it is debited to your credit card, currency fluctuations could change the overall price.

Does the item have a guarantee?

Not all foreign guarantees are valid in the UK, so check carefully with the retailer before committing yourself. Also find out whether you'll have to return the goods to the supplier's country if they're faulty. There may be an affiliated supplier in the UK you could go to for repairs instead.

Can you trust the retailer?

Buying from a retailer you've never heard of and haven't checked out is a dangerous business. Stick to retail sites you know have a good reputation. You can see what other shoppers have had to say at review sites such as **Bizrate** (www.bizrate.com) and **The Public Eye** (www.thepubliceye. com). Or you can seek advice and news from the **National**

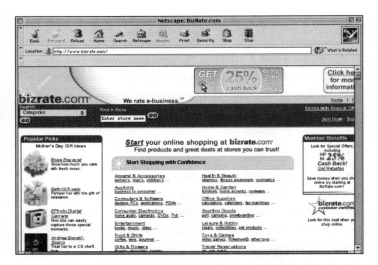

If you're not sure about a retail site, you can find out what other shoppers have had to say about it at review sites such as Bizrate (www.bizrate.com).

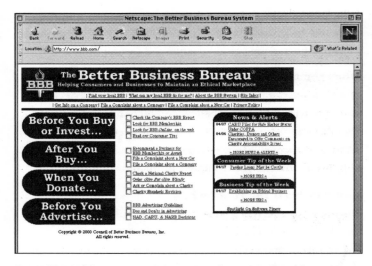

Better Business Bureau is a ratings services that vets websites for security and reliability.

Consumers' League (www.natlconsumersleague.org). There are also various ratings services, such as the **Better Business Bureau** (www.bbb.com) and **WebAssured** (www.webassured. com), that vet websites for security and reliability. Look for security 'kitemarks', too, from the likes of VeriSign and TrustE.

Do you know where the retailer is based?
Disreputable retailers can often disguise their true country of origin simply by providing false information on the website. And even if you do know where they're based, the purchase contract may be governed by the laws of the country that actually supplied the goods, which is not always the same. If you felt forced to take legal action you might have to do so in the retailer's home country. This is clearly impractical and potentially very expensive.

Does the site offer secure ordering?
By now it goes without saying that you should only send your credit details across a secure (encrypted) connection (*see* **Safe Shopping**, *page 21* for more on this).

Will the retailer offer good customer service?
When you order online good retailers will give you a unique order confirmation number and follow-up e-mails keeping you updated about the progress of your order. Find out what the site's customer service practices are before buying. There's usually plenty of information in the 'Frequently Asked Questions' and 'Help' sections of reputable websites.

Paying by credit card

As mentioned in Chapter 3, paying by credit card can give you added protection should the foreign retailer go bust or fail to deliver the goods. Although the major UK card issuers refuse to accept that the Consumer Credit Act applies to cross-border transactions, they do tend to accept liability on a voluntary basis, but only up to the amount of credit provided.

Sorting out problems

Buying abroad is fine when things go right – you can net yourself a bargain. But if things turn nasty, getting them sorted out can be a real headache. Language barriers, distance and different consumer protection laws can complicate procedures to the extent that you feel like giving up.

If you are unhappy with the service you've received, complain first to the retailer and keep copies of all your correspondence. If this gets you nowhere, you can turn to the following organizations for help:

Euroguichets
These are consumer advice organizations co-funded by the European Commission. Their primary aim is to help sort out cross-border consumer complaints originating in their own countries. There are Euroguichets in France, Luxembourg, Spain, Republic of Ireland, Greece, Italy and Germany. In the UK, the Euroguichet service is provided by the national Citizens Advice Bureaux. Have a look at the **National Association of Citizens Advice Bureaux** (**www.nacab.org.uk**) website for more information.

International Marketing Supervision Network –
www.imsnricc.org
This is a worldwide network of consumer protection agencies. The UK's **Office of Fair Trading** (**www.oft.gov.uk**) is a member. There is a voluntary system to help resolve cross-border consumer complaints. If you complain to the OFT it can pass on your complaint to the relevant overseas agency for their attention.

Have a look at the National Association of Citizens Advice Bureaux (www.nacab.org.uk) website for information about Euroguichets.

The European Advertising Standards Alliance –
www.easa-alliance.org

EASA is an alliance of 22 advertising regulatory bodies across Europe, including the UK's Advertising Standards Authority (ASA). It operates a cross-border complaints procedure such that if you're unhappy with the claims made in a foreign-sourced advert, you can complain to the **ASA** (**ww.asa.org.uk**). It will contact its fellow organizations to try to get the matter sorted out.

Legal action

Only consider legal action as a very last resort. The rules are extremely complicated and you are unlikely to get your legal fees back even if you win your case. For more

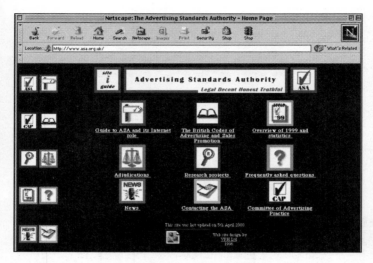

The UK's Advertising Standards Authority (ASA) operates a cross-border complaints procedure.

information on your rights in this area, go to the online shopping advice section of the OFT's website.

The future

The EU is introducing a number of directives aimed at unifying consumer rights across Europe, the most relevant being the European Union Distance Selling Directive, scheduled to become law in June 2000. It will include a seven-day statutory cooling-off period after you've received the goods. You can return the goods within that period and get a full refund.

Other directives will give consumers, amongst other things, statutory rights of repair or replacement for at least two years from the date of delivery of the goods. If these aren't possible you may be entitled to a discount or a full refund.

Although we're doing quite well harmonizing consumer protection law in Europe, it doesn't help much given that most foreign online shopping is done at US websites. We're still a long, long way from agreeing an international set of standards. So until then, it's up to you to protect yourself. There are bargains to be had, but no-one would blame you for concluding that the risks of shopping abroad outweigh the benefits.

Chapter 7

The Future

These are early days for shopping online, and yet things are moving very fast. There are technological changes afoot that will enhance the online shopping experience immeasurably. Here's a brief summary of the main developments.

Unlimited net access

First we had the revolution that ushered in free subscriptions to internet service providers, pioneered by Freeserve. Then attention focused on the cost of telephone calls. So now ISPs, cable companies and telephone operators are all beginning to offer unlimited net access for fixed monthly or annual fees. This means you won't have to worry about how long you're spending online any more – you can surf away all day if you like without paying a penny more.

Of course, all these companies seem determined to make things as complicated as possible, introducing different tariffs according to whether you're a light or heavy net user, and insisting on using particular telephone companies for your voice calls and so on. Some of them seem incapable of introducing a new service without adding bells and whistles. Competition will be intense, though, as more players enter the market, and prices are bound to fall. This will give a massive boost to online shopping, as surfers feel they can spend longer online.

Faster connections

At the moment, the fastest conventional modem speed is 56 kilobits per second. That's not really fast enough for viewing live video demonstrations or hearing flawless streaming audio. Software and graphics-rich websites take ages to download. But, at last, new high-speed services are being introduced, such as Asynchronous Digital Subscriber Line (ADSL) and cable modems, capable of transferring digital data at 10 to 50 times faster than our current modems can manage. Again, this new technology is unlikely to be cheap at first, but the price will undoubtedly fall as it gains wider acceptance.

Faster connections will greatly enhance the quality of the services online retailers can offer. Auctioneers will be able to provide mini-videos of auction lots, allowing bidders to take a good look around sculptures and antique furniture. At the moment, two-dimensional pictures aren't really good enough to sell three-dimensional objects. This technology will help fashion retailers, too, as customers will be able to download videos of people modelling clothes. We'll be able to see them from all angles and feel more confident about buying online. Before too long we may even be able to look at virtual models of ourselves and see how the clothes suit us...

Digital interactive television

Shopping via the television is already taking off in a big way thanks to the success of the two digital television platforms, Open and OnDigital. Subscribers can access a number of retailers and buy online, using the remote control and special set-top boxes plugged into their televisions. Soon digital interactive services will be fed into our living rooms via cable, satellite or through TV aerials.

Television, formerly an entirely passive medium, is being transformed into an interactive transactional one. Viewers will be able to respond directly to adverts and buy products there and then if they want. We're unlikely to be offered full net access through our televisions though, largely because service providers might be held liable if people accessed the kind of illegal or offensive content that is widely available on the web. Such activities could break current UK broadcasting rules. So providers are offering a selection of retail, financial and entertainment services within a controlled environment known as a 'walled garden'.

So although the PC is no longer the sole access point for net services such as e-mail, banking and shopping, digital interactive television won't replace it, just complement it. Although interactive television has had a good start, it will take a few years before the technology beds down and it achieves mass distribution. The problem is that there are far too many competing technologies at the moment requiring too many confusing set-top boxes and so on. And with digital televisions only just replacing analogue versions and Digital Versatile Disks taking over from video tapes, home entertainment technology is in such a state of flux, many people are holding off buying anything until it all settles down and prices begin to fall.

Shopping on the move

The rise of Wireless Application Protocol – a new standard for transmitting net data to mobile phones, hand-held organizers and pagers – is a significant change in the relatively short history of the net. For the first time it means that people can access online services very easily whilst on the move. There's no need to plug a laptop into a telephone socket any more. You can view redesigned and simplified web pages on your WAP phone screen.

Imagine you're browsing in a high-street shop and you're thinking of buying a particular product. Normally, the impulse to buy would probably stop you from shopping around to see if you could find the same product cheaper elsewhere. Being lazy, you also don't want to put in the leg-work.

With WAP phones you can just make a simple call to an online price comparison service and it will do the shopping around for you. It could reveal that a shop nearby offers a much better deal, show you a mini map of how to get there, and even give you the opportunity to buy the product online there and then via a secure encrypted link. All you would need to do then is saunter over to the shop and pick up your purchase, mulling over potential uses for the savings you've just made. Perhaps you'd like to go to a film or a concert? You simply get online to an entertainment booking service, browse the latest listings, book tickets and even choose your seat positions, all using your phone or hand-held organizer.

And with the imminent widespread adoption of Bluetooth, a wireless standard that enables digital gadgets to communicate with each other over short distances, we won't need wires dangling about all over the place. We'll probably be wearing miniature microphones in our lapels than can transfer voice commands to WAP phones safely tucked away in a pocket or briefcase. If you have headphones, you could listen to your ISP's latest entertainment recommendations or your shopping portal's latest online bargains.

Once voice-recognition software is perfected, we'll be able to shop on the move extremely efficiently, without even having to look at whatever digital gadget we've chosen. After all, we don't have to see CDs before we buy them, or wine for that matter. We will simply tell our voice-activated gadget to get online and go to particular websites that will then talk to us about their products and special offers. I know this all sounds a bit *Blake's Seven*, and this kind of technology won't be with us tomorrow, but it will come sooner than we think.

We're rapidly moving towards an 'anything, any time, anywhere' market – net access via any number of gadgets, at home or on the move. Before too long the net will cease to be talked about because everything will be online. It will become so pervasive that people will forget all about the underlying technology. That indifference will be the sign of the net's ultimate success.

Intelligent agents

We've already seen in Chapter 4 (**Useful Starting Points,** *page 45*) that the future of online shopping belongs to the shopping portal sites incorporating highly sophisticated price comparison search engines. At the moment these still require us to enter the name of a product into a search box and off they go trying to find the best price for that product. But soon they will be advanced enough to suggest purchases to us before we've even thought of buying them.

For example, suppose your car insurance is coming up for renewal. If you've completed an online application form giving all the usual details – previous claims, make and model of the car, number of years no claims discount and so on – your intelligent shopping agent could scour all the motor insurers collecting quotes for you and simply tell you which one offers the best deal. All you would have to do is say whether or not you wanted to accept the quote, press one button and buy the insurance. Your payment details could already be stored securely on your PC or with the intelligent agent's website. Imagine all the time, effort and money that this kind of service could save you. This idea could obviously be extended to all your other household bills.

And if you've always been interested in buying a second-hand Jensen Interceptor sports car, you could program your intelligent shopping agent to scour all the motor websites, including auctions, looking for one. Some months later you might get an e-mail telling you that it has found one in pristine condition being sold by a female octogenarian tee-totaller from the Isle of Man.

The only disadvantage, of course, is that if you make shopping around more efficient for one person, you'll generally make it more efficient for everyone with access to the same technology. This means that bargain-hunters will automatically face stiffer competition from fellow bargain-hunters. There's very little chance of keeping something secret on the web once intelligent agents begin scurrying around at the speed of light. But they still promise to transform online shopping.

Retail websites are already targeting e-mail news bulletins at people whose tastes and previous purchase histories they know. Some may view this as intrusive, but as long as you have control over how much information websites can collate about you, this kind of targeting can prove very useful. After all, it's far more annoying having to wade through e-mail telling you about the latest speed metal CD releases if you're only interested in Vaughan Williams.

Future payment methods

Most online payments are currently made using credit or debit cards. These are fine for relatively large payments, but not very cost-effective for payments under £5, say. New online retailers can be charged 1.5% to 2% per transaction by card operating companies, such as Visa and Mastercard. But there is a big potential market for low-cost services requiring so-called micropayments. Transferring money across the banking system is expensive at the best of times, so collecting micropayments has been a non-starter for many small retailers.

And yet there are many services that web retailers would dearly love to charge for and we'd probably be happy to pay for. Some examples. Imagine you're desperately looking for a flat to rent on a classified ads website. You want to be ahead of the pack, so you might be prepared to pay 50p, say, for one-off access to the very latest ads tucked away on a protected part of the website. Or say you want to download the latest single from your favourite band – you'll quite happily pay the few pounds that might cost. What if you've just got off the plane and you need somewhere to stay the night? You access a hotel reservation service using your WAP phone. The service finds you a room nearby and lets you book online. You're quite happy to pay a small fee for that, too.

How do the web service providers collect such small sums of money without having to absorb losses processing credit and debit card transactions? The likely answer is that they do away with cards altogether and just use the telephone billing system instead. This can be done via PC or via mobile device. There are solutions coming on to the market that involve online shoppers being given a number to ring and a code number that they tap in using the telephone keypad. Once the number has been accepted the website confirms this and proceeds with the transaction. The cost of the purchase is added to your telephone bill. There are no cards involved.

Handling online credit card payments poses security problems for retailers, too. Verifying the identity of cardholders is difficult. How does a retailer know that the credit card details given haven't been stolen, especially if the required delivery address is different from the billing address? Online retailers also have to put in stringent security measures to protect card details from hackers. This takes time and money. Anything that does away with the need for cards should prove popular.

This kind of billing system will have a big impact on mobile e-commerce as well. Mobile phone operators could find themselves handling payments for a whole range of web retailers charging for services accessed by mobile phone users. Supposing you're in the pub and you want to find out the latest football score. You could log on to your favourite sports website, make the request and be charged 20p for the privilege. You see the purchase itemized on your phone bill or maybe on a separate bill that lists just your online transactions. In Finland you can already pay for Coca-Cola, car washes and even golf balls this way. How the retailers collect the money from the phone companies is up to them, the online shopper doesn't have to worry about it any more.

And it won't be just be micropayments that WAP phones will be able to handle. Before long, the small card that contains the microchip inside mobile phones (SIM card) will also be able to contain our digital signatures. We'll be able to buy cars and other expensive goods over the web using our WAP phones to pay via a highly secure encrypted link.

Other online payment technologies, usually involving some kind of 'cyber coin' or other digital cash equivalent have so far proved too complicated to gain wide acceptance. One stumbling block has been the lack of consumer demand for such technology. Why should we be in favour of something that enables web retailers to start charging for services we've been getting for free?

Other solutions involving 'electronic purse' smartcards, such as Mondex, that you load with digital cash, have also had a hard time getting established because of the need for swipe-machine gadgets to be incorporated into computers or at least linked up to them.

What we might see is an extension of the loyalty cards, favoured by supermarkets and petrol stations, for online payments. There's no reason why these companies couldn't start exchanging points for a wider range of consumer products and services. Another way round the expense of collecting small credit card payments is for websites to give customers a tab that they run up. When it reaches a cost-effective level the retailer debits the account. Alternatively customers could pre-pay a larger sum and then use the service on an ad hoc basis until their credit is used up.

Chapter 8

Site Guide

Some internet guides seem to be nothing more than long lists of website addresses. This guide is different. So many new retailers are launching online these days that such lists go out of date very quickly. There are plenty of sites (such as those mentioned in Chapter 4, **Useful Starting Points**, *page 45*) much better equipped to keep lists current and provide ratings for ease-of-use and security. The main function of a guide like this is to give you the tools and the knowledge to shop online securely and with confidence, no matter what new sites or technologies come along.

Anyway, it is my firm belief that the future belongs to the online shopping portals and price comparison engines. If you want to buy a CD, you could just go to one of the retailers recommended below. But surely you're far better off using a site that will find you the cheapest place to buy that CD? (*See* Chapter 4.)

There are exceptions to this, of course. If you like the clothes of a particular fashion designer, only his or her website will do. Similarly with other unique items, like designer jewellery or furniture. So if you're after something or someone in particular and the website isn't listed in this

If your looking for someone or something in particular, try searching for them using a search engine such as Copernic (www.copernic.com, above), Google (www.google.com, below) or good old Yellow Pages (www.yell.co.uk, opposite page).

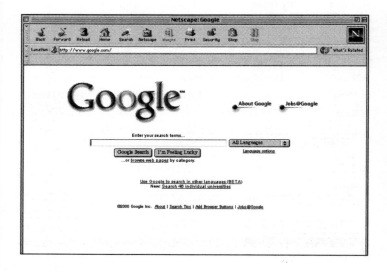

guide, you'll have to resort to good old-fashioned search engines and directories.

Here are a few good ones to try (mostly UK-based):

AltaVista UK	**www.altavista.co.uk**
Copernic	**www.copernic.com**
Excite UK	**www.excite.co.uk**
Google	**www.google.com**
HotBot	**http://hotbot.lycos.com**
Yahoo! UK	**http://uk.yahoo.com**
UKOnline	**www.ukonline.com**
What's Online	**www.whatsonline.co.uk**
UK Plus	**www.ukplus.co.uk**
Search UK	**www.searchuk.com**
UK Max	**www.ukmax.com**
UK Directory	**www.ukdirectory.co.uk**
Yellow Pages	**www.yell.co.uk**
Scoot	**www.scoot.com**
BT PhoneNet UK	
(directory enquiries)	**www.bt.com/phonenetuk**

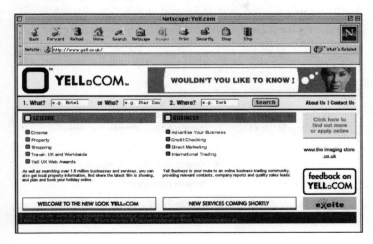

Some useful websites

The websites listed below are a subjective selection intended merely to point you in the right direction. You may have your favourites, I have mine. They are mostly UK-based, with some US sites thrown in for comparison. In some categories there weren't many sites I could wholeheartedly recommend. For example, the clothes sector still has a long way to go to offer a truly satisfying online shopping experience in my view, but it is getting better.

No one website is best at everything. The cheapest site may not be the best at customer

> **TIPS**
>
> *As long as you follow the advice given in this book about safe shopping, you should be able to make your own informed assessments of good and bad sites.*

service and vice versa. You may simply hate the design of one website and prefer another, even though it comes less highly recommended. But as long as you follow the advice in Chapter 3, (*see page 21*) about safe shopping, you should be able to make your own informed assessments of good and bad sites.

Department stores and catalogues

Argos	**www.argos.co.uk**
Bloomingdales (US)	**www.bloomingdales.com**
Harrods	**www.harrods.co.uk**
John Lewis	**www.johnlewis.co.uk**
Macy's (US)	**www.macys.com**
Shoppers Universe (US)	**www.shoppersuniverse.com**
Shopping.com (US)	**www.shopping.com**

Reccomended UK department stores and catalogues include Argos (www.argos.co.uk, top) and John Lewis (www.johnlewis.co.uk, bottom).

If you want to visit a US department store, try Macy's at www.macys.com, above or Shoppers Universe at www.shoppersuniverse.com, below.

You can buy books online at the Blackwells site (www.blackwells.co.uk).

Books

Alphabet Street	www.alphabetstreet.com
Amazon	www.amazon.co.uk
Barnes & Noble (US)	www.bn.com
Blackwells	www.blackwells.co.uk
Bookpages	www.bookpages.com
BOL	www.uk.bol.com
Dillons	www.dillons.co.uk
Internet Bookshop	www.internetbookshop.co.uk
Waterstone's	www.waterstones.co.uk
W H Smith	www.whsmith.co.uk

Music, video and DVD

101CD	www.101cd.com
Amazon	www.amazon.co.uk
Blackstar (video & DVD only)	www.blackstar.co.uk
Boxman	www.boxman.co.uk

Buy CDs at 101CD (www.101cd.com, above) or CD Paradise (www.cdparadise.com, below) and clothes at Cafe Coton (www.cafecoton.co.uk, opposite page).

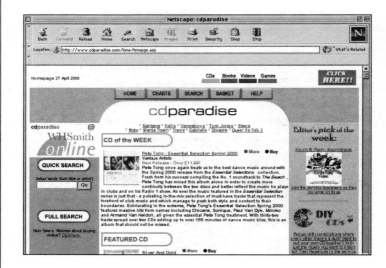

CDNow (US)	www.cdnow.com
CD Paradise	www.cdparadise.com
CD Universe (US)	www.cduniverse.com
HMV	www.hmv.co.uk
Entertainment Express	www.entexpress.com
Virgin Megastore	www.virginmega.com

Clothes and fashion

Boden	www.boden.co.uk
Boo	www.boo.com
BrasDirect	www.brasdirect.co.uk
Cafe Coton	www.cafecoton.co.uk
Charles Tyrwhitt	www.ctshirts.co.uk
Diesel	www.diesel.co.uk
Easyshop	www.easyshop.co.uk
Freemans	www.freemans.co.uk
Intofashion.com	www.intofashion.com
Kays	www.kaysnet.co.uk

Fashion shops such as Diesel now offer an online service.

Redoute	www.redoute.co.uk
The Shirt Press	www.shirt-press.co.uk
Zercon	www.zercon.com
Zoom	www.zoom.com

Food

Asda	www.asda.co.uk
Fortnum & Mason	www.fortnumandmason.co.uk
Jack Scaife	www.jackscaife.co.uk
Lobster	www.lobster.co.uk
Organics Direct	www.organicsdirect.co.uk
Safeway	www.safeway.co.uk
Sainsbury's	www.sainsburys.co.uk
Simply Organic	www.simplyorganic.net
Somerfield	www.somerfield.co.uk
Tesco	www.tesco.co.uk

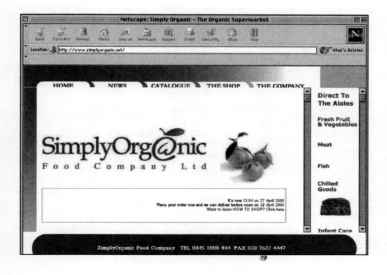

There are a number of specialist food sites, such as Lobster (above), which offers gourmet food, and Simply Organic (below), where you can buy organic products.

Online off-licences Orgasmic Wines (www.orgasmicwines.com, above) and
Beers Direct (www.beersdirect.com, below).

Wine & beer

AmiVin	www.amivin.com
Beers Direct	www.beersdirect.com
Berry Bros & Rudd	www.bbr.co.uk
Bordeaux Direct	www.bordeauxdirect.co.uk
Chateau Online	www.chateauonline.co.uk
Drinks-Direct	www.drinks-direct.co.uk
Mad About Wine	www.madaboutwine.com
Only Fine Beer	www.onlyfinebeer.co.uk
Orgasmic Wines	www.orgasmicwines.com
Waitrose Direct	www.waitrosedirect.co.uk

Toys and computer games

Early Learning Centre	www.elc.co.uk
eToys	www.etoys.co.uk
Funstore.co.uk	www.funstore.co.uk
Games Paradise	www.gamesparadise.com
Gameplay.com	www.gameplay.com
Hamleys	www.hamleys.co.uk
Internet Gift Store	www.internetgiftstore.co.uk
Jungle.com	www.jungle.com
Lego	www.lego.com
Toyzone	www.toyzone.co.uk
Toys R Us	www.toysrus.co.uk

Computers

Apple	www.apple.com/uk
Compaq	www.compaq.co.uk
Dell	www.dell.co.uk
Dixons	www.dixons.co.uk
Egghead.com (US)	www.egghead.com
Hi-Grade	www.higrade.com
Jungle.com	www.jungle.com
Simply Computers	www.simply.co.uk

Buy toys at Funstore.co.uk.

There are hundreds of websites supplying computer hardware and software.

121

Whether your looking for the best sounds or action...

Software

Download.com (US)	**www.download.com**
Microwarehouse	**www.microwarehouse.co.uk**
PC World	**www.pcworld.co.uk**
Simply Computers	**www.simply.co.uk**
Software Warehouse	**www.software-warehouse.co.uk**

Consumer electronics and home appliances

21Store	**www.21store.com**
Argos	**www.argos.co.uk**
Be Direct	**www.bedirect.co.uk**
Carphone Warehouse	**www.carphonewarehouse.com**
Comet	**www.comet.co.uk**
Dixons	**www.dixons.co.uk**
DVD World	**www.dvdworld.co.uk**
Go Digital	**www.godigital.co.uk**
Home Electrical Direct	**www.hed.co.uk**
Quality Electrical Direct	**www.qed-uk.com**
Richer Sounds	**www.richersounds.com**

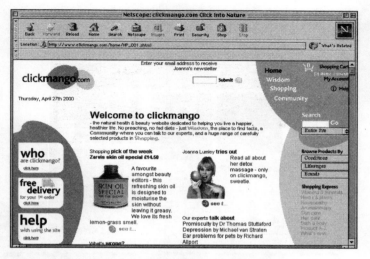

...or just trying to make yourself beautiful, you can usually find what you need on the web.

Unbeatable	**www.unbeatable.co.uk**
Value Direct	**www.value-direct.co.uk**

Health and beauty

Academy Health	**www.academyhealth.com**
Allbeautyproducts.com	**www.allbeautyproducts.com**
Allpharmacy	**www.allpharmacy.com**
Boots	**www.boots.co.uk**
Clickmango	**www.clickmango.com**
Pharmacy2U	**www.pharmacy2u.co.uk**
The Body Shop	**www.thebodyshop.co.uk**

Art & antiques

Artnet.com (US)	**www.artnet.com**
Axis	**www.axiartists.org.uk**
eBay	**www.ebay.com** or
	www.ebay.co.uk
GavelNet (US)	**www.gavelnet.com**

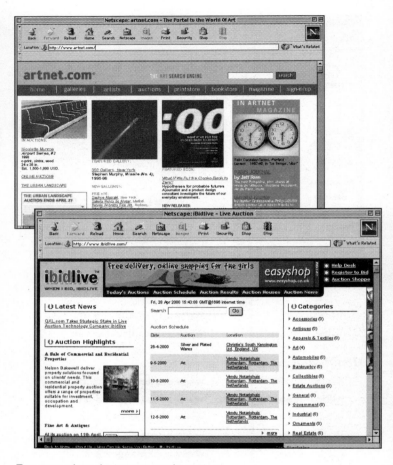

Two areas where the internet excels: auctions…

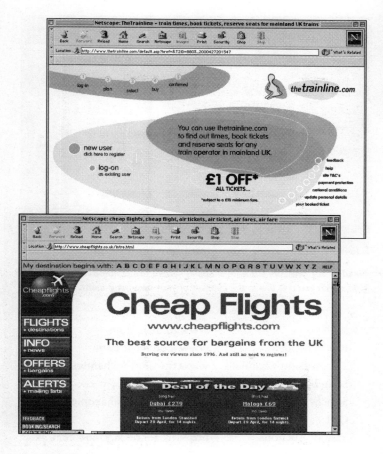

...and travel.

Need to buy presents but hate shopping? There are hundreds of ideas for gifts, which you can buy in the comfort of your own living room.

IbidLive	**www.ibidlive.com**
ICollector (US)	**www.icollector.com**
The Auction Channel	**www.theauctionchannel.com**
Sotheby's.com (US)	**www.sothebys.com**
Sotheby's-Amazon.com (US)	**www.sothebys.amazon.com**
QXL	**www.qxl.com**
Yahoo! Auctions	**http://uk.auctions.yahoo.com/uk**

Travel

A2B Travel	**www.a2b.com**
Bargain Holidays	**www.bargainholidays.co.uk**
Cheap Flights	**www.cheapflights.co.uk**
Dial-a-Flight	**www.dial-a-flight.com**
Ebookers	**www.ebookers.co.uk**
Expedia	**www.expedia.co.uk**
Lastminute.com	**www.lastminute.com**
The Trainline.com	**www.thetrainline.com**

Index